Also by Perry L. Angle

Existential Musing of a Southern Individualist
Existential Ramblings of a Southern Individualist
Prophet's Way
The Waiting Room Chronicles
The Butterfly Transport

In this book,
all commentary simply reflects the opinion of the author
based upon his many years of involvement in sales,
management and investments.

AN INVESTMENT PRIMER FOR NEW INVESTORS

A Step-by-Step Guide to Investment Success

PERRY L. ANGLE

iUniverse, Inc.
Bloomington

AN INVESTMENT PRIMER FOR NEW INVESTORS
A Step-by-Step Guide to Investment Success

iUniverse books may be ordered through booksellers or by contacting:

iUniverse
1663 Liberty Drive
Bloomington, IN 47403
www.iuniverse.com
1-800-Authors (1-800-288-4677)

ISBN: 978-1-4759-3418-2 (sc)
ISBN: 978-1-4759-3419-9 (e)

Library of Congress Control Number: 2012912073

Printed in the United States of America

iUniverse rev. date: 7/5/2012

DEDICATION

For Ginny, Kim, Brian, Craig &
my grandchildren
and for all new investors who are just beginning their
investment journey.

My Qualifications

MBA Auburn University Licensed Stockbroker in Practice
for 22 Years

First Million Dollar Salesman in My Product Line

Regional Manager for a Fortune 500 company

Traded most types of financial instruments

I can help new investors because I have the academic
training and sales and managerial experience necessary to
explain both market fluctuations and strategy.

Introduction

I wanted to write this investment primer for new investors to illustrate the common sense principles that helped me to become a successful stockbroker. This is a complex subject, and it is easy to get lost in the many opportunities that the various markets offer to the investor. A common sense approach will enable the reader to maneuver through an array of fundamental and technical considerations relative to an investment choice.

You will learn to use research, have a limited but useful understanding of economics as it relates to investments, select among available strategies and, most importantly, learn to rely on your own judgment. At the onset you will recognize the important difference between speculation and investment. Speculation may accidently be profitable at times, but a well defined investment program invites success.

If you are the self starter for whom this book is written, you will not be equipped with the knowledge that I refer to as investment mechanics. This will come later and we will learn enough to begin. Experience will augment your knowledge as we progress.

We will start with a simplified case study of two fictitious companies, XYZ and AYK. At the end of this primer, you will be able to make a reasoned choice as to which of these companies offers the greatest chance for profit. Remember, you will be doing the exact same thing when you become an active investor.

Even the best experts make mistakes in weighing the relative merits of a stock or bond or other investment. Yes, I have made such mistakes. You will as well. A mistake is a learning experience and the very best advisors in the business have made many such errors, but they learn to avoid the same faults in future judgments. That is why they become known as investment pros.

Have faith in yourself. Confidence, not arrogance, makes a successful investor. I will also give you some hints on how to select a broker when that time comes for you. All the charts, formulas, mathematics, etc that you will learn to use will follow. Your first job as an investor is to learn the mind set or framework for study. This was worth more to me in my career than all the necessary peripheral mechanics that I learned to use. That is where we will start.

I thank you for allowing me to help you understand and appreciate investments. Let's begin.

CAUTION

This book is an introduction to a broad and complex subject. When you have finished the book, you will have an understanding of many principles that will lead to your success in investment selection. You will learn about the undercurrents that permeate the markets which are usually related to economic or political considerations. Supply and demand is foremost among these matters.

What you will gain from this survey is the framework crucial to your decision marking abilities. I will introduce you to some of the tools you must have to begin such as knowledge of the current ratio & P.E. ratio –the mechanics. I will examine charting and explain why a proper assessment will include both fundamental and technical analysis.

Keep caution in mind at all times. Learn this material.

CONTENTS

PART ONE
MIND SET PRINCIPLES

Through the past you gain experience
for the present, but swiftly it morphs to the future.
This is where your dreams reside.
Today is your starting point.

ECONOMICS AND THE BUSINESS CYCLE

Websites on the internet will give you many definitions of economics. Let's simplify explanation and use my personal definition. I define economics as the study of what makes commodities worth more or less in the marketplace. I speak of commodities as things you use or are used to produce the things that you use such as corn, cotton, coffee, cement, orange juice, gold etc and yes, even money.

Some have referred to this discipline as the "dismal science". Not so! It is vibrant, exciting, changing and explanatory. The great economists, Milton Friedman, Hayek, Lord Keynes, Adam Smith and others offered theories as to how economies grow. It can be a bit daunting. I remember trying to explain the principles of this study to my daughter in high school. I started by talking about efficient markets, portfolio theory, and later realized I should have begun simply with common sense applications.

My daughter is a homemaker now and uses economics everyday as do your parents. Let me give you an example.

Her family likes orange juice, and a hard freeze hit the Florida orange groves. She knew enough of the effect of that on supply and demand to understand that price would probably rise. So she went to the store that day and bought cans of frozen orange juice. It was a smart move and a move most moms would make without deliberation. That is economics in action.

What can we learn from this? Supply and demand are linked in the thought processes of homemakers and not surprisingly in the world of stocks and bonds. I will suggest this simply based on my college training. Price is the point at which supply and demand best meet i.e. price represents equilibrium between the two. Thus, price is what we pay for an item or investment. Supply is how much of it is available, and demand is how much of it is wanted in the marketplace.

Basic supply and demand for any commodity (including money) will control price. Expect price to rise or fall with changes in the two. I am indebted to the economist or person who thought of money as a commodity as it makes the explanation of some economic outcomes easier.

So how would you change price for an item or investment?

1. By making less of it (supply).

2. By wanting less of it (demand).

3. By finding a product that works better (obsolescence).

4. By finding out that the product is not as good as intended (relevance).

CRUCIAL POINT FOR THE BEGINNER

Most of economics is concerned with supply and demand.

Use common sense to understand economics as it relates to investments. Worry about the refinements in theory later.

Any group of economists given the same data to analyze will not likely arrive at a consensus opinion. Why? Value judgments as they relate to markets are a matter of interpretation. Will Rodgers once said, "An economist's guess is liable to be as good as anyone else's." Perhaps, but the economist has the knowledge to make a more accurate opinion on the value of the data than the uninformed. Therefore, I urge you to understand economics in the larger sense. Don't get mired in the details.

The Business Cycle

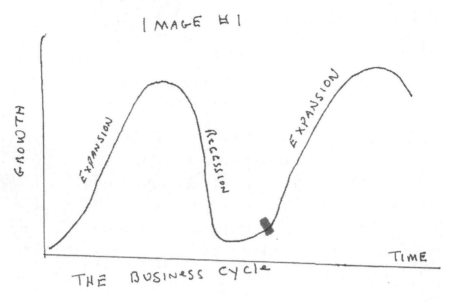

I have always found it useful to have a mental picture of the business cycle. I usually make a mark where I think the market is on the curve. On the y axis of a graph is growth and on the x axis is time. The cycle is nothing more than a series of troughs and peaks. If I think that we are at the top of a peak, I anticipate a coming decline. If I believe we are at the bottom of a trough, I will expect a rebound. History suggests that there will always be alternating peaks of expansion and recession within a cycle. You get a heads up by knowing an approximate point on the curve. It is a necessary ingredient for planning.

Incidentally, the products that serve you well in an expansion will probably hurt you in a recession, so it is useful to know which products fit which point on the curve. Another way is to think that different investments will fit inflationary expectations (expansion) and different ones will work best in deflationary times (deflation).

AT A TROUGH ANTICIPATING AN EXPANSION	AT A PEAK EXPECTING A DECLINE
Precious metals, Energy, Equities	Bonds and utilities

POINT: As long as capitalism fosters a business cycle there will be bull and bear markets. Bull markets go up and bear markets go down.

Inflation and Deflation

Inflation is a general rise in prices of goods and services. Most economists now believe that the cause of inflation is related to an increase in the money supply. Thus it becomes important to consider money as a commodity. This prescient idea was suggested by an economist, but I am not sure of the source. Think of wheat or corn and consider that a general rise in the supply of these items will cause the price of that item to fall. In the same manner, an increase in the money supply would cause the purchasing power of the dollar to decline. This would be inflationary.

Deflation is a general decline in prices caused by a severe reduction in demand for goods and services. Deflationary or recessionary periods may result in a rise in unemployment. Another side effect is a general decline in spirit or a negative wealth effect. The 1930's in the United States was such a period and saw the worst form of deflation, called a depression.

Remember:

Inflation will suggest investments of necessity first. Inflation will usually cause noticeable adverse price changes for commodities and will cause a decline in the purchasing power of the dollar. Inflation may lead to substantial political unrest (as will severe deflation). Also in these hard times expect changes in the supply and demand equation for any item.

Later, when you have time try to learn the basic theories of economics. I refer to the Monetarist School, the Keynesian School and the Austrian School of economics. Each was honored by one or more luminary figures. Several were Nobel Prize recipients.

Out of control inflation can lead to hyperinflation which is what occurred in Germany in the 1920's and recently in Zimbabwe. The last 2008 issue of a 100 trillion dollar bill is the worst example to come to mind of hyperinflation where the inflation rate at one time hit 500 billion %. I know the figure seems incredible. Hyperinflation and depression are polar opposites of monetary policy and are marked by economic and political distress.

In the period from 1925-1998, the annual rate of inflation was about 3.1%. Rules of measurement have changed since then and the true real rate of inflation can only be guessed at today. Possible signs of deflation include the onset of 0% financing on high cost items, low money market and savings rates and a general loss of consumer confidence.

The classic definition of inflation is too much money chasing too few goods. Monetary authorities have injected an incredible amount of money into the system in an attempt to keep us out of recession or depression. This is a typical inflationary move designed specifically to combat a deflationary problem. If this designed move fails, then a depression could become a reality. That is not likely, but possible. The boom-bust, inflation-deflation, and bump about, are normal consequences of the business cycle.

REMEMBER that inflation is a result of changes in money supply and that interest rates are not a cause of inflation but are an effect.

I was born in 1941. Television got started then, labor negotiations begin in earnest, Pearl Harbor was attacked and life expectancy was almost 63 years. Gasoline was 12 cents/gallon, a postage stamp was three cents and sugar was about six cents/pound. The Red Ryder b-b gun was a big Christmas item.

To see the ruinous effect of long term inflation simply look at the price of these items now compared to 1941. This horrid loss of purchasing power is one reason for the world's growing disregard for the dollar as a reserve currency.

One of economics most interesting dilemmas is the gun-butter problem as it relates to governance of the populace. Say hypothetically speaking that the government has only 100 dollars to use to divide between guns or butter i.e. between defense and food. We will assume that use of the printing press is not an option to augment the 100 bucks. The choices are to devote $100 to defense and none to food or to allocate $100 to food and none to defense or to make some other arbitrary division of the resource. In short, the government must choose between guns or butter. This real life dilemma also happens every day when retiree's must decide between food and medicine. You can see that nothing is more integral to your understanding of market behavior than economics.

The One Hundred Trillion Dollar Bill

Hyperinflation is considered to be caused by increases in the money supply such that the purchasing power of the currency declines and prices for goods and services increase. Of course, the opposite of hyperinflation is depression. Many countries have went down this road including China, Germany (Weimer republic in 1923), France, Hungry and most recently Zimbabwe in 2008. Surprisingly the United

States has been a victim with the continental dollar and the Civil War greenback.

Since the United States debt was devalued I can't help but wonder are we headed that way again.

ETHICS, ETIQUETTE AND SUBJECT KNOWLEDGE

When we speak of investing, what idea first comes to mind? Normally, the "market" is the one referenced and by inference that usually means the stock market. Know that within the stock market are a number of markets however; the Dow Jones Industrial Average is the first consideration. The DJIA is an average of thirty industrial stocks. You should know that there is also a Dow Jones Utility Average and a Dow Jones Transportation Average. Let's stay with the industrial average for now.

There can be many subdivisions within each market as with the stock market. I mentioned the three averages which are watched closely, also closed end funds, ETF's, MLP's and more, but for simplicity sake let's stay generic and discuss stock (also called equities) in general. But while we confine ourselves to the stock market for now, please know there are bond markets, commodity markets, precious metal markets and others as well.

The Stock Market

First, we need to understand what a stock is. It is an evidence of ownership. Let's say for instance that dad gives you a share of Disney for your birthday. You will then own a pretty piece of paper that says you own one share of the company and as an owner you will have certain rights, such as the right to receive dividends and a right to vote on company matters unless the stock is non-voting, etc. Yes, one share would be a very small part of the whole. Even so, you are still an owner. All the certificate does is serve notice to the company that you are an owner (stockholder). Thus you become one among many.

What is the difference between a stock and a bond? Now suppose that instead of a stock your parents give you a Disney bond. What do you have? Simply stated, it is a piece of paper that identifies you as a bondholder entitled to be paid interest by the company. Note: with a bond you get income that is called interest as opposed to dividends that could come with the stock, and the fundamental difference is that you are a creditor as opposed to an owner i.e. because you own the bond you have actually lent the company money and the company lists you on their books as a debt holder. One last big difference is that, if the company went bankrupt you as a bondholder have a better claim on any remaining assets.

Stockholder	Bondholder
Gets dividends	Gets interest
An owner of the company	A creditor of the company
Lower claim on assets	Better claim on assets

Those who desire a more secure income stream might want to be bondholders and those who prefer growth of their assets will choose to be stockholders. Now that we understand the differences let's get back to stocks (equities) in general.

I want to give you an example of what I mean by knowing your subject. To know the Disney stock you would need to know what Disney does, where it is located, who its competitors are, are they solvent (can the company pay its bills) and more. These are fundamental factors and important to your decision. Also, we would need to look at the technical situation which we will discuss later.

As a young broker I made some mistakes in that I did not research my company as well as I should have. Once, I recommended to an important client that he buy a cosmetics company. I based that decision solely on an observation that some of its employees drove distinctive looking cars and assumed that the company was doing well. It wasn't and my client lost his money and I lost my client. MY BIG MISTAKE was that I knew nothing about cosmetics. I had no fundamental or technical reason to make that recommendation. I DID NOT KNOW MY SUBJECT. I consider that one of the best lessons I ever learned. Know your subject well enough to be confident in the recommendation.

Ethics and Etiquette

Ethics is the study of moral issues, behavioral expectations and essentially the Golden Rule standard. Is there a place for ethics in the fast-paced world of investable situations? (The answer is simply when is ethics not applicable to general conduct especially in zero-sum game situations?) We can trace the subject back to the early philosophers such as Aristotle.

Any investor will agree there is no place for an unethical broker, and I would add there is no place for an investor with the same orientation. Some of the first thinkers argued that ethics was one of the disciplines that taught one how to best live. It should be. So treat your broker with kindness and be mindful of all he had to learn in order to provide the services you seek. Be respectful to him and expect the same.

Etiquette

Your workplace may have a published or unpublished set of expectations as to manners. Things you should not do. You wouldn't wear inappropriate attire in a business setting or chew gum at a business session. Also remember that what might be considered acceptable in this country might not be in another. If you have foreign friends or clients, you need to understand their culture. You want to be punctual and arrive on time and not leave early from the workplace. The Boy Scout Oath is an excellent guideline for behavior. A glance at Robert's Rules of Order might also be useful. As a broker, I learned that the next client who came to me might be a challenge from a morals or manners perspective. I needed to work within common sense boundaries. So will you.

Please be careful to guard your comments in public and especially online. There are legal considerations known as slander and libel. The new investor for whom this book is written needs to become familiar with these terms.

INVESTMENT REVELANCY

By this I mean: Is it useful? Is it necessary to a particular industry or is it a necessary component of some product? Is it as indispensable as air, water, or salt? If it is none of these things, why would we have an interest? Perhaps, it is some object that appeals to us such as collectibles (coins, art, and entertainment). Any of these may be relevant to us and justify a purchase. Where's the danger? It could be a fad some passing fancy that may bloom and then fade away or some toy that is the rage and may lose its appeal in the following year.

Here is what we need to know about relevance: All products have a life cycle from an economic standpoint. Do we expect the appeal to last a few weeks, months, years or a very long time? Products that are expected to continue in vogue for a long time tend to hold their relevance longer. For instance the horseshoe helped to expand the west but now has a much more limited usage.

Obsolescence is the killer. If it can be replicated and is subject to competition you must expect obsolescence. Take for instance Beta, VHS, DVD's and now Blue-Ray. This marketplace is always changing because of technology. You must always factor the potential for obsolescence into your decision making. Also remember that any product can be reverse engineered which will enable competitors to design a similar product. This occurs even in the presence of patent protection.

Ask Yourself: Will My Choice Be Quick To Obsolesce

Investment traps

Pyramid and Ponzi schemes

These schemes involve paying off new investors with the very funds that came from the initial investors. A Ponzi scheme usually promises a high rate of return normally unattainable in the marketplace, and that is a real clue to this fraud. As long as the new investor funds the exchange of money to the other investors, this type of scheme may continue. In 2008, a long standing Ponzi scheme made national headlines. Beware!

Here is what you look for: Unregistered securities, strange looking account statements, reluctance to mail checks when asked, and general evasiveness. Also, if your contact is not appropriately licensed then you can be certain of trouble.

A pyramid scheme is similar and may actually involve a product. You might be asked to become a distributor. The product may be real or supposed.

No doubt you have heard, "If it sounds too good to be true, it probably isn't true." Indeed!

Stay within the framework of the established marketplaces. Please!

POSITION IN THE WORLD
& POSITION IN THE GROUP

Your natural American pride may lead you to think that in any given year the U.S will be the dominant world market. Actually that has happened but not as often as you might expect. The U.S. is only a fraction of the world marketplace, something close to a third, perhaps.

So, if you limit your investing horizon to just the U.S. then you may be missing two thirds of the opportunity. I have always advocated having some foreign exposure in my portfolio. I am sure that you can think of many household brands of foreign companies that trade here either by themselves or as ADR's or foreign ETF's.

Another way to get foreign exposure is to select a top quality fund manager who offers foreign mutual funds. A mutual fund can be a good first choice for a young investor. No doubt that we are a leader in the world but bear in mind that in the investing world we compete with emerging markets, frontier markets and others.

What might make a country tops in any year may be political or economic or by some gain in competitive advantage. Be aware of the domino effect that such an event in one country may affect on others. So it pays to keep your eye on world events.

I liken it to the often expressed idea of the Butterfly Effect in Chaos theory. The theory suggests that a butterfly flapping its wings in one place may cause a change of events in another. It is a bit wild as theories go but it is colorful and does suggest that world events are often interconnected.

RETIREMENT

What you don't have one? If your answer is that you are young and just beginning to invest, I can't agree. If you have made any income, it might be a great time to take a little and set up a Roth Ira. There are several types. The traditional IRA is tax-deductible (with some restrictions). The Roth Ira is not deductible but the earnings accumulate tax free after five years and if withdrawn after 59 ½. A 10% penalty may apply if withdrawn before then. The great advantage of an IRA is the compounding. Don't be late in starting an IRA. A wonderful old maxim is to pay yourself first. This is one way to maximize your late years earning power.

A study was done some years ago by the Social Security Administration which said that out of 100 people at age 65 only one was wealthy, 54 were broke, 34 were dead and four were well off. I doubt that the facts have changed much over the years. Your best hope for a retirement is to begin now with a traditional or Roth IRA.

This study was reinforced by a Department of Labor survey in 1998 which said that 5 people out of 100 would have enough to live on in retirement. It said 28 would depend on welfare, charity or social security just to survive. I wonder if that statistic isn't higher now.

Remember the Boy Scout motto "Be Prepared"? Sound advice! You should start planning for retirement now. Why not take your first three profits and start an Ira?

Always remember the warning which any good company should repeat to you. Past performance is no guarantee of success.

The Roth Ira is one of the few real contributions to personal finance which the congress has given us. You can make non-deductible contributions up to 100% of earned income before the tax deadline. Withdrawals are permitted but may be subject to a 10% penalty if taken before age 59 ½. Some no penalty distributions are permitted due to death or disability. The best provision is that no required minimum distribution need be made at age 70 ½. This is a major advantage over the deductible IRA.

RESEARCH AND TAX CONSIDERATIONS

Remember, a guess is an investment dead end.

An overall appreciation of the current environment is required. Thus to be a student of the market means being a student of current events and, to a lesser extent, of financial history. Here is how I would approach research:

1. Do I consider the world situation relatively stable?

2. Are there any countries I absolutely would avoid?

If so, be wary of ETF and mutual fund concentrations of this country.

3. What are my predominant investments objectives?

   Growth, Income, Short Term Trading, Hedge

4. What investment product best fits my primary objective?

5. What asset allocation shall I use with my available funds?

    Bonds x %, equities y %, cash z % other a%

6. If I choose equities and growth what companies do I select?

    Same question for other choices

7. Do the fundaments support my choice?

8. Does the chart support the fundamental recommendation?

Now we have a plan.

I like to read some financial publications to give me additional viewpoints. I will tell you some of my favorites are *Barron's, Investor's Business Daily, Money, Forbes,* and a number of individual research publications. In my opinion, for an all- around excellent assessment of almost any investment question, I favor the weekly publication, *Barron's.*

In my opinion, the best publications will use technical charts, in depth articles of product interest, stock, bond, ETF and mutual fund price tables, insider transactions and knowledgeable discussions among selected panels of well known investors. One problem with these publications is that the mail can delay receipt. You must develop similar interfaces with the computer. I don't actively trade commodities anymore but the commodity sections can give you a clue as to the usage of basic materials essential to a growing economy. That is why I watch copper so closely.

DO THE RESEARCH. YOU WILL
BE RICHER FOR IT

Unsolicited Mail

Another useful source of research is the so called "Junk Mail". It will be unrequested, perhaps even unrelated to personal objectives and arrives usually in spurts which coincide with turning points in the market. I always look at unsolicited financial pieces for clues. For instance, when I last saw a temporary top in the precious metals market, it was foreshadowed by increasing advertisements to buy gold and silver. Often you will see signs in the windows of various financial and jewelry stores to buy your scrap pieces. And the inevitable hotel sessions which promise to pay a "fair price" for the items. Don't fall for it.

When I was writing this book, the following types of junk mail arrived.

"The Secret Destruction of Paper Money"

"Secure Your 30-day Food Reserve"

"Why a Towering New Uranium Boom Is Near"

"The Mother of All Financial Bubbles Is Just Now Starting to Pop"

"Mushrooming Government Capabilities to Control Society"

The uranium claim is interesting because an argument can be made on both sides, and the same plea was made when I was a broker in 1999. This one seems to surface with the precious metals scares. "Buy now or you will regret it" is the underlying theme. All I can say is that I am glad I didn't fall for any of these errant wisdoms in 1999. And very few folks want a nuclear reactor in their back yard especially after Chernobyl, Three Mile Island and the recent disaster in Japan.

Nevertheless, this type of mail can open your eyes to the worst case scenario and that is its real value. Some nuggets of wisdom can be gleaned from the doomsayers. Junk mail can offer ideas about change in sentiment. I have found some real profitable stocks by projecting out from the worst case.

Look at your junk mail. It is research. This type of wakeup call seldom appeals to the optimist viewpoint but that doesn't lessen its value. I actually paid to receive the last statement about the efforts to control our lives and it scares me most (the "big brother" is watching you idea). It suggests a revisit of the ideas in Orwell's Animal Farm.

Tax Considerations

You will come to understand a lot of tax related subjects such as capital gains, wash sales, qualified dividends, tax deferral etc. All this will come. First please recall that our objective is to make profits, so I believe that the tax issue is secondary.

Let me put it another way. The tax should be the tail on the dog, not the entire dog. NEVER, and I repeat NEVER, base your profit or loss decision entirely upon the tax question. Say you have a large gain in XYZ stock and the market looks to turn sour. So you say to yourself, "I can't sell because I would have to pay such a large capital gain." If the stock profit is in danger it should be sold or hedged by writing a covered call or buying a put. To allow a loss by indecision is not a sound strategy.

However, in one instance you would have to pay close attention to the tax question. That would occur if the profit is near the capital gain threshold of one year and a day. You would want to cross that time boundary in order to gain a lower tax on the profit.

PSYCHOLOGICAL FACTORS

DIVERSIFICATION AND THE EIGHTH WONDER
(And a comment or two on needs versus wants)

You want to be right, need to be right, hope to be right. Why? All of us want to be winners and it is human nature to be confident in yourself. Yet, there is a difference between want and need. Needing to be right implies an aggressiveness that may prove harmful. Wanting to be right in investment selection is a lot safer platform to stand on than need.

A lot of psychology is involved daily in the markets. Stocks go up and down because of shifts in sentiment. You will hear the terms fear and greed. Both are normal and necessary consequences from expectations of sentiment changes. What changes sentiment? Such events as geopolitical events, economic events, changes in climate i.e. catastrophic situations such as the great drought in the Midwest in 2011, or the floods in Thailand in the same year will all qualify. One way to watch for change in this important indicator is to use charts, i.e. technical analysis. We will look more at charting as we go on.

Approach the market in the proper manner. Say I want to win and behave like a smart chess player. Realize that every action you take will suggest a future action. Ask yourself before placing that order: Is this the best opportunity I see for now and the immediate future? Is sentiment on my side? Have I made an attempt to research this investment using both fundamental and technical tools?

Timing

A famous investor named Sir John Templeton, founder of the Templeton funds, once cited a study where in theory one bought at every high for a period of time and another bought at every low for the same period. Naturally, you would expect that the fellow who bought at the low did much better.

Not so much difference as you would expect. The results were fairly close. I don't remember the exact words, but I think Sir. John's conclusion was that what really mattered was time in the market and not trying to time the market. He knew what all good stockbrokers and even amateurs learn. No one can accurately predict the exact highs and lows of the market.

If we want to get complicated, we could look at seasonality, cycles and indicators but for now let's lean on the basics. Start with the fundamentals of the investment, i.e. the products, the competitors, the company controllers, etc. Next, learn to use the most basic technical tool which is a simple chart. When I think of timing, I think of length for instance the length of my supposed involvement with the stock or bond. I have this in mind before I buy and also have in mind a target that I hope the investment will achieve. Know this, please.

You can hold an investment too long and see it crash down like a spent satellite or you might not hold it long enough and then miss the potential. In short, based upon your research, project a mental target range and be prepared to sell at your high point and buy at your low point.

Volatility

Markets change direction quickly and often violently. For no apparent reason a market may go from up to down in free fall fashion as it did in the crash of October 1987. There is a measure of volatility now called the VIX. This volatility index is used by traders to evaluate the level of complacency in the market. Normally it will trade between 20 and 30.

< 20   some apparent calmness in attitude

> 30   indicates some fear and nervousness.

(It can be used to indicate a contrarian move.)

At 30 I might look for a pullback <20 I may consider a bottom

Another measure of individual stock volatility is called the Beta. A so called normal beta of one would suggest that your stock will move in tune with the market. A beta of two would be twice as volatile and you would expect faster moves in either direction. You should know the beta of the stock you are buying as it will give you some feel for the risk of that issue.

Some volatility is caused by High Frequency Trading using sophisticated mathematical algorisms. This accounts for the large volume swings that seem so unfair to many investors. It is certain that large computers can focus on fleeting opportunities that small investors cannot. Some counter with the argument that such trading adds liquidity to the marketplace and indirectly benefits the small investor.

It is my opinion that the few advantages cited are minor compared to the fact that the individual does not have instantaneous access to the same information flow. The real danger occurs when the computers malfunction or are mis-programmed. This can cause a sudden change in the markets, a situation comparable to the famous "flash crash event". This potentiality makes your job of fundamental and technical research even more important.

Let me tell you about a really bad day. I had been a broker for twelve years when the market crashed in 1987. That day will always be imprinted upon my mind and I am reminded of it when I see froth in the marketplace and computer malfunctions such as happened on the day of the Facebook debut.

The 1987 freefall began, accelerated and, by the end of the day, wiped out many small investors. I could not believe what I saw unfolding on my computer screen. Later, one of my clients called and asked me, "What was it like?" I answered that it was like the Kid Shellen scene in the movie *Cat Ballou*. In that scene, Kid Shellen was drunk and was sitting on his horse. He was leaning against a building wall for support. A young boy said something like, "Kid; you ought to see how bad your eyes look."

Kid Shellen replied, "You ought to see them from my side."

That scene best describes my feeling on that horrid day. You had to have seen it from my side. No explanation could justify that sinking feeling and the aftermath of trying to explain this irrational volatility and panic to my clients. You just had to have seen it from my eyes.

Diversification

(NO PRINCIPLE IS MORE SOUNDLY GROUNDED IN EXPERIENCE)

You should have investments across asset classes and with different managers if concentrated in mutual funds. A real danger exists with asset concentration. Do not put "All your eggs in one basket." Examples of failed companies whose employees lost their IRA's and 401k's due to bankruptcy are legend. Even if you work for a great company that offers an attractive employer match, do not fail to invest outside the company.

Flexibility

You should have most of your investments in products that are easily exchanged or sold. The essence of flexibility is to be able to adjust with a minimum of effort or cost.

The Eighth Wonder

The eighth wonder has been called Compound Interest. If you have X dollars earning interest (money market funds, saving accounts etc.) and interest is added to original principal as is subsequent interest (without withdrawals) then you are compounding, i.e. P+I then I, then I, becomes P+ 3 I where each previous interest payment is helping to compound the next. This is the simple consideration of compounding. Reinvesting of dividends can have a similar effect.

Dividends (the good and bad signs)

I like dividends. As a stockholder, you are an owner and entitled to remuneration. Some companies plow earnings back into the company coffers (for R&D, employee benefits or employer grants--options). The board may send up a smoke screen called buybacks. The idea is that XYZ retrieves shares on the open market and thus raise earnings per share. However, if they misuse the retired shares through employee stock options then the benefit is lost.

My preference for dividends reflects the fact that I control the distribution. When you look at a company profile for its dividend policy, be sure that the dividend is covered, i.e. that the earnings per share (EPS) completely covers the proposed payout. Also beware of dividends far in excess of an industry standard. You should also look at the financials and especially the current ratio to check for solvency.

A good place to shop for solid dividend plays is in the dividend payment section of *Barron's* or other financial publications.

Risk and a Low Profile

The wise trader knows that risk attends every choice.

You probably already know about risk. If you played in sports, you know that risk is a part of the game. So expect it now but no need to fear as it will come in many forms and soon you will recognize most of them. Here are a few.

Reinvestment risk

This risk exists because you must do something with the investment. Perhaps it is a bond you hold that matures or is called away by the issuer. Let's say you were getting paid 6 % a year in interest. However, when you go to reinvest the proceeds you find that the going rate for a comparable bond is only 4%. Your income stream is now compromised. This happens a lot in fixed income investments and is especially hard on retirees.

Tax Risk

Here is a easily understood risk. Not to worry, as you can't do much about it. If congress changes the tax code it can disrupt the intent of the investment you hold. In the Tax Shelter years, that is exactly what occurred. Suddenly, tax shelters did not have the same shine to them and people lost heavily. A number of good books were written during this period.

This is a sad story to relate about the heyday of tax shelters. Certain tax breaks were available to investors who bought positions in real estate ventures, public storage, and oil and gas packaged products.

I was reluctant to sell these but was under considerable pressure as a broker and at the onset no one could be certain that the statements made in the prospectus were true. However, to describe the risk is the mission of the prospectus which was given to each investor. Not many took the time to read and understand those risks.

I did sell a very few of these that seemed to have real promise and I tried to get my investors to attend company sponsored seminars. I begged them to read the prospectus and told them that there were certain risks.

This was a painful time in my career as all of these investments failed. In one instance, a shopping center tax shelter came to the attention of my branch manager. The anchor tenants were located near my home. The boss told me, "Sell this thing. It is right in your backyard." The fact that the shopping center was near a dog track was, in his mind, a big plus.

One Saturday, I went and parked my car in the parking lot and stayed for most of the day. The traffic was very low. It was apparent to me that even after the grand opening this was a bad deal. I refused to sell it and it went under. The Branch Manger was not happy.

Congress changed the tax laws and the great advantage of tax shelters as a packaged product disappeared. Also, it became apparent that many of the shelters never properly invested the monies received. Elaborate artist renditions of planned communities which had appeared in some prospectus were never even built. This painful personal experience was proof of the real danger of tax risk. If governments wish to take away a gift they can and will. A simple revision of the tax law is all that is needed to devastate the investor.

Geo-political Risk

World events change market momentum. Let's say you own shares of an oil company in South America and a new regime nationalizes the company. It will probably cause a sharp reversal. Egypt caused some disruption to the oil market (supply concern). Keep an eye on world events that affect your investments.

Governmental approval risk

This can be a huge problem in the medical device and pharmaceutical areas. A promising drug could fail in final phase three trials and have to be withdrawn from the market at a large loss of time and expense.

Obsolescence or new product development risk

If your product is dependent upon technology, be vigilant for change. New product developments by the competition can upstage your investment. This is why you will want to know what your company's competitors are doing. What does their pipeline in development look like? This is an important risk to understand.

New Account Form Risk

This is not a risk of your investment but of your participation in the markets. You will be asked to sign some forms which tell the broker much about you. Be careful what you check off on the form. For instance, if you check speculation as an objective and wind up in an arbitration proceeding or conflict over your objectives, speculation may hinder your chances to win. Understand speculation may have a place but only when you gain the knowledge necessary to appreciate the nuances of the marketplace. Also, be careful of the income category. Don't try to impress anyone on this form. Tell the absolute truth about your income and your objectives but don't embellish them.

Identity Risk (Identity Theft)

Strictly, this is an associated risk and not an investment risk. It occurs because of the manner that you choose to dispose of unneeded documents. Identity theft is the fastest growing crime in America. I took every precaution, yet it happened to me. When you establish a presence on the internet even under a supposed safe site you have left a footprint. Similarly when you receive documents in the mail you have a paper trail. When no longer needed, you should shred these documents in a cross cut paper shredder. Remember that criminals are some of the smartest people in the world. Leave nothing of importance in your trash. Most of the time identity risk occurs because you were careless with your personal information.

Destroy all personal information no longer useful to you in a secure manner.

Migrant Broker Risk

This is risk you take if you follow your broker to another firm. Transferring your account is not difficult. If you choose to follow your broker in his transfer, you should satisfy yourself by research that it is of his choosing, that he is not being asked to leave. It would not be unusual for a broker to make a career move as I did however, more than one move in a career should be cause for concern.

This is a horror story which actually happened. I was close to a man who liked his broker and when the broker left, he followed. The problem is that the broker left many times and at short intervals. Later, the man found out that there were reasons for this mobility and, despite numerous appeals the man came to his senses and did not follow. Often, but not always, a broker who is excessively mobile has compliance issues and should be avoided.

You must know that the broker is motivated to make money for the firm. Of course, to accomplish this in theory he must make money for you (or you might leave him). Often there are incentives given to the broker to recommend a certain type of investment. I will state that there is much less of that now than when I was a broker but it will behoove you to be on the lookout for those incentives. If the product seems outside your stated objectives be sure to ask if the broker is getting extra compensation.

Asset Allocation Risk

This is the classic "too many eggs in one basket" risk. It is a failure to properly diversify across asset classes.

Currency Risk

This is the risk of translation of earnings from one country to another as in the case of taking U.S. foreign earnings for XYZ brands back into U.S. dollars. Currencies can revalue daily, thus the risk.

LOW PROFILE (Mum's the Word)

My father was a man who believed in keeping a low profile. He thought that the less people knew of his financial affairs the better he would be. As a man in his 90's, it made sense. But it was a philosophy that he adopted as a child of the depression. Often he was without food and took any work he could find in order to support his mother and sisters. He even fought bare knuckle in the alleyways to earn small prize money. Mum's the word remained the proper strategy for all of his life.

I was not as careful to keep private my financial affairs until later in life when I reluctantly realized that my father was right. This is a world where exploitation is common. You are often reminded of some horror story almost daily in the news where some person was hoodwinked into buying repairs that they did not need, or talked into paving a driveway and then halfway through the company would raise the price. These people were probably targeted because someone thought that they had the ability to pay. In many cases, the unfortunate person paid in advance and seldom got references or checked the better business bureau.

It's a matter of preference, but I will not use debit cards or ATM machines out of privacy concerns. Over the years I have warmed up to dad's idea of keeping a low profile and that includes not telling friends or relatives about your financial affairs. Your best friend or near relative may tell someone who doesn't need to know and that could bring you grief.

Now and for later please remember when you make a lot of money in the stock market stay low. Mum's the operative word.

FUNDAMENTAL VERSUS TECHINICAL

For the purposes of this chapter we are going to create a fictitious company called PQRS. As we gather information we will list what we have learned in a table. Table 1 shall be called PQRS fundamentals. Our questions are as follows: What does the company do or make? Who buys the product i.e. the target market? Our company is a medical device company which makes a portable EKG machine which is used in small doctors' offices and clinics.

PQRS FUNCAMENTALS
Medical Device Company
The product is an EKG machine
Sells to small medical offices and clinics

Here are some further points to ponder. There are few competitors in this space. Unfortunately, PQRS does not carry a significant backlog of orders. The current ratio is 1.6 which indicates it is paying its current bills. The manager has been with the company since it was founded in 1980 and receives stock options and a salary of 6 million per year. His sister is the secretary and his brother is vice president and both get salaries of 2 million per year. Two other relatives are officers but the Chief Financial Officer is not a member of the family.

We need to know how much the product costs to make and what is its retail price? The answer is the EKG retails for $800 per unit and has a manufacturing cost of $300 per unit. Obviously one of our key previous concerns is satisfied. The product is relevant because it is a diagnostic tool in use for a major health problem. In this small niche, the product should not obsolesce too quickly.

PQRS FUNDAMENTALS TABLE

High compensation paid to officers.   Largely family owned and operated   -CR is 1.6

Product in use in small medical settings   Medical device company----No meaningful order backlog

I realize that we are building a fictitious company seemingly in an aimless fashion. Be patient, there is method here. Soon you will know enough to make a tentative assessment of investment potential. Let's assume our cost accounting is complete and we determine a breakeven point (BEP) for the product. If we add in normal sales expenses, taxes, insurance, supplies and benefits to the manufacturing cost we come up with $650 per unit. We also need to know that the company size is 600 million (an abbreviated example of capitalization). Now let's finalize our chart.

Finally we learn that the company operates only in the U.S. and Mexico. It sold 2000 units last year. It pays no dividend to shareholders and issues no earnings guidance.

The company has only 150 employees. Long term debt is substantial for a company this size and will began to mature in two years.

PRQS FUNDAMENTALS TABLE (2)

Medical device company	Sales BEP point 650/unit.	Family owned and operated
No meaningful order backlog	CR is 1.6	Highly paid officers
Sell to small offices and clinics	Company size is 600 million dollars	Company has few active competitors
It sold 2000 units last year	Each unit sells for 800/unit	It has 150 employees
The product is manufactured in Mexico.	No dividend and no earnings guidance.	Substantial long term debt.

Let's make one half of our decision now. Why one half? It is because we have to take a look at the technical picture. Not a lot of good stuff here. No!

The Technical Picture

There are points that I like and I defer a final decision to the chart. First, what is it that troubles me from a fundamental standpoint? The product fits a good target market space and that is important because it may set a barrier to the big guys who may not want to spend substantial dollars on a small market. For the moment the company is solvent (Cr =1.6) but the large amount of long term debt that comes due in two years is of some real concern.

Most disturbing is the fact that it is largely family owned and the company pays its officers outrageous salaries for the size of the company. Especially so, when we consider that the shareholder gets nothing. And with no earnings guidance from year to year how will the investor anticipate profitability from quarter to quarter. This may practically account for the absence of a real order backlog.

This exercise was intended to get you in the mind set of evaluating a variable. You must learn to analyze the data available to you. If you do not give just due to fundamental analysis you will make mistakes. Let's look at the chart for PQRS and see if that helps us to finalize our decision.

Technical Analysis

I like technical analysis because I believe the premise is sound. Technicians believe that everything that happens to or is known about a company is immediately incorporated into its price. Thus, by examination of the chart you can get a sense of the urgency of your decision. Most commodities trade by technical analysis and a good broker will have a grasp of it.

There are several kinds of charts. Time periods vary but it is generally true that the most complete picture is found with a longer term chart. I differ in this respect. I look at a one year chart and then consider a three month chart.

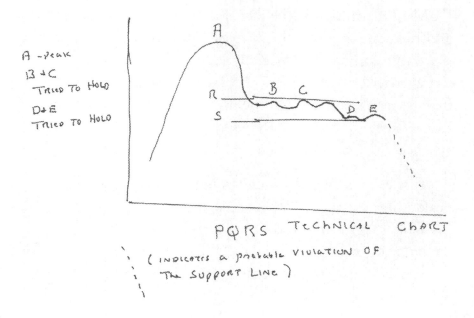

A –peak
B &C
  Tried to hold
D & E
Tried to hold

R
B   C
S
                    D E

PQRS Technical Chart
(indicates a probable violation of
the support line)

Obviously this chart doesn't look good. A glance tells us that the company is losing momentum. It reached its peak in the present cycle at A, ran into hesitancy at B-C, tried to hold at D-E but broke down again. R is the resistance line and S is the support line. Note the dash line is support violation.

I have made my decision using both fundamental and technical analysis. PQRS is not for me. This is how we approach a decision to invest. Look first at the fundamentals then at the technical picture.

| FUNDAMENTAL | tells | What to buy | (or sell) |
| TECHNICAL | tells | When to buy | (or sell) |

One of the first ideas you need to visit in technical analysis is what does the chart suggest about the future direction of the stock. Without getting too deep here, you should be able to decide whether you have a continuation or a reversal pattern. This can be seen with any type of chart. Here are some guidelines.

CONTINUATION PATTERN	REVERSAL PATTERN
Wedge Flag Pennant	Head and Shoulders, Hanging Man
Some types of gaps Triangles	Double top, double bottom, Doji

For this purpose my favorite chart is the Candlestick chart. It was invented well over four hundred years ago by a famous Japanese rice trader. Candlesticks are rectangles that are color coded as to direction. I believe that this chart pattern gives better clues as to changes in sentiment than any other chart type.

Technical Indicators

Moving Average

This represents the average price of the issue over a stated period of time. The line gives a smoothed out picture of the overall direction. I would tend to sell if the stock would be likely to break below its moving average and be quick to buy if it appeared that it would break above that average. I usually look at the 50 and 200 day moving averages.

Relative Strength Indicator

The RSI offers a picture of the internal strength of the stock. The tendency is to buy with a strong RSI and to sell if it appears that it will break down.

Bollinger Bands

This useful technical tool frames the price action of the stock between two boundary lines. When the two lines tend to move toward each other, expect a movement in that direction. The bands are marked by standard deviation measures.

On Balance Volume (OBV)

The OBV technique came into more general use in the 1960's and was championed by Joseph Granville. It adds and subtracts volume to arrive at a single total volume figure which is continuously updated. The resulting line gives an idea of the true trend that is in place. It should be used in conjunction with other momentum indicators.

These indicators will help you understand the overall price action of the stock.

COSTS OF DOING BUSINESS

Many types of costs are associated with investing in the various markets. First, let me list a few here then target a couple for consideration.

12b-1 fee	Commission Costs	Surrender fees	Advisory fees
Handling fees	Company paid fees	Margin costs	

And a not often considered, kind of quasi-cost is called Opportunity Cost.

Opportunity Costs

Perhaps this is the most important cost because if you learn to mentally evaluate your alternatives this must come to mind and its understanding will make you a better investor. PREMIS: ALL INVESTMENT ALTERNATIVES HAVE A COST INCLUDING BOTH THOSE CHOSEN AND THOSE IGNORED.

Opportunity cost is simply an attempt to value the next best alternative that you did not select. You can think of many examples, such as a cattleman deciding between raising cattle or hogs. If he chooses hogs and cattle prices soar, then his opportunity cost would be the equivalent value of the lost revenue from not raising cattle. In our case, a choice between a bond and a stock might clarify the idea. Say we choose between a bond with a yield of 2% and a stock with a yield of 5%. For illustration we ignore commission costs, safety issues, etc. The opportunity cost of the best alternative sacrificed if we choose the bond is 3% i.e., 5% less 2%.

You must consider this idea when investing. What is the cost of the best alternative to your current choice? This is important whether you chose between companies or types of bonds. Everything has a cost, even the next best alternative.

Commission Costs

For planning purposes I would figure 3% as a normal cost. It does vary.

The Advisory Fee

This is a business management fee charged by the brokerage house on the amount of assets that you have on account. The basic idea is that by doing this you pay less in ongoing commissions. On a large account that excuse may have some validity. You must evaluate the fee carefully. Listen to this horror story.

Mr. X came to me and asked for my help. His account had been even to down for a long time despite an ongoing up market. The person was 71 years old and was on a fixed income which was somewhat dependent on earnings from the account. I did not believe that the size of the account warranted an advisory fee. I was right. In addition, the majority of the funds were growth oriented which would have been more appropriate for a younger person. It was also not a well diversified account as most investments were of a single type. I explained this to Mr. X but he seemed annoyed at me for pointing out the reason he was losing. I thought of the ancient days when it was common to shoot the messenger.

The truth was that the advisory fee charged quarterly was taking almost 80% of the entire income from the securities. The broker had a continuing stream of income at the expense of the account holder.

If there had been any validity to the idea that the advisory fee would lower the overall cost as new purchases were made, that was completely lost as a value because the account was 100% invested in longer term securities. So the support shelter offered by the ongoing advisory fee was worthless.

Company Paid fees

These fees are usually very small and more often found in direct investments between you and the company itself. They can be nice to have but may add to your taxable basis in the shares. For instance, let's say you set up a direct investment account with XYZ Company itself then the company may pay some incidental fees under the heading company paid fee.

Comments On Fees

Commission costs will vary with the amount of the investment. The per unit cost should decline with the more shares you purchase. The costs may vary with the type of investment. This is an item you should immediately clarify with your broker. It is considered normal to ask for some discount if you plan on trading stocks to any extent and he should be willing to consider your request.

Online trading may involve a stated per transaction fee (true with many websites). In general, you should expect that you may be asked to pay postage and handling fees. I have always thought that should be a part of the stated commission fee but you may not win that argument.

12b-1 fees (Mutual Fund Fee)

This unpopular levy can be in addition to load charges. Since it is based on total assets it is called an asset-based sales charge. The idea behind this charge is that it is said to reward brokers for their ongoing assistance to the customer who buys the fund. In truth, there are few additional briefings by the broker as these types of assets are long term holdings. Every prospectus will disclose and explain the fee and should be read by the investor.

As a broker, I liked to receive these fees and felt they were at least partially justified for the after the sale service I tried to give the client. However, now with a different perspective I can understand the consumer dissatisfaction.

Surrender fees and Transfer fees.

I call these the "penalty for leaving me fees." These might include the declining surrender charge which can occur during the first few years of an annuity or the transfer fees for transferring from one broker to another.

Velocity of Money

This term refers to a measure of the rate of change of funds. Think of a river in constant motion (check out the famous quote of Heraclitus). So does money move through an economy or through your hands. In finance, it can give you an idea of the strength of an economy. In your case consider that stagnant money (money employed in a low rate of return situation) may not offer the best possible return. Always remember that safety has a cost. It is necessary, surely, but it can be costly if you recall the comments on Opportunity cost.

Margin

In a margin account, the investor can use his portfolio as collateral for stock purchases at a percent of the current market price. Today that requirement is 50% and is set by the Federal Reserve under their regulation T. The period just before the stock market crash of 1929 had much lower requirements. In fact, at one point securities could be bought on margin for as little as 10% down. Some theorists believe that contributed to the Great Depression. The Federal Reserve does not often change this figure but it is one of their tools.

If the stock you buy with margin goes down, you will receive a margin call which must be met in a timely manner. It will be necessary for you to deposit securities or cash in an amount to meet the 50% margin requirement. For the beginner I would seriously discourage the use of margin.

ESCAPE PLANNING

―――――――――――――――――――――――――――――――――――――

ESCAPE FROM WHAT?

Any of these possibilities may be cause to reconsider an action or a position in the markets.

From a broker with whom you have issues
From a brokerage house that changes its policies
From a stock or bond position that is no longer reliable
From your own original investment philosophy that is not working.
From insurance coverage issues that arise to question in the relative time frame.

Dead Horse Stragedy

When one of my investments is not going my way or when disillusioned with brokerage house changes to policy, I think of the old Sioux Indian solution.

When you are riding a dead horse,
the best idea is to dismount.

An escape plan should begin with your purchase plan. You need to know what assets you have that would not be transferable from one broker to another. Ordinarily, I would avoid these. An example might be in-house funds, i.e. broker DDD's own company funds. If you decided to leave DDD you might find that his funds would not transfer and you would have to liquidate at a possible loss. Stay with investments that are widely known and accepted at all brokers.

INFLUENCE OF THE FED

History relates a number of financial problems leading up to the Great Depression. Bank panics occurred with some regularity. To help to control the banking system, a central bank entity called The Federal Reserve System was created in 1913. (I remind the reader that the business cycle was a contributing factor with the troughs and peaks in economic activity).

The Federal Reserve was given a "dual mandate" which was to moderate interest rates and inflation by creating a stable employment base. Since 1913, the Fed's duties have increased in keeping with the difficult job of regulating the nation's monetary base insofar as their techniques permit.

All we need to know now is that the Fed has considerable influence over the behavior of the markets and the Fed has a number of adjustment tools that can be used such as changing the reserve requirements for banks or changing the margin requirements for investors.

The new investor needs only to know this as a beginner. The marketplace will be dramatically affected by the Fed's overall bias toward a loose or tight money supply.

MAXIMS

These are sayings that you will often hear expressed in a trading environment.

The Market Climbs a Wall of Worry Sell in May and Go Away

Buy on the Rumor and Sell on the News

These statements are not always true. You will hear them so I thought I would introduce them to you. The market does seem to climb a wall of worry as in 2010-2012. There were many unusual and dangerous happenings and the market could have panicked. There were down days but it recovered. The idea of selling in May refers simply to the fact that the majority of gains in the market seem to come roughly from November to May. That, of course, is not an absolute.

I can recall two recent examples of what I consider to be affirmations of the "Buy on the Rumor and Sell on the News". The first involves the initial public offering of the much hyped Facebook. On May 18, 2012, Facebook came to market and was expected to run up and settle at a price much higher than the offering price of $38 per share. Initially, it did run higher but closed at $38.23. This company had a 900 million user base but did not live up to its promise on the first day. This illustrates the often erratic behavior of new issue initial offerings.

I do not favor IPO's as an investment for these reasons:

1. Often the stock opens with no actual trading history as an exchange based equity and will have no reliable chart pattern.

2. Insiders and those who would flip the stock (buy as a quick profit speculation rather than an investment) will sell at the first opportunity.

3. A new issue will often be followed by additional offerings which will dilute the earnings per share.

The simple fact is that this much anticipated initial offering of a well known stock was an embarrassment to the company and to its sponsors. Frantic trading of the stock had an effect upon the electronic tracking system. This highlights a real concern which I have about the advantage given to accelerated trading by computers.

The second example is what happened with Lion's Gate. This is a media company which has an extensive movie and TV title library. It was the company that had the *Hunger Games* movie. Before the movie was released the stock rose to its recent high. The movie was expected to be a blockbuster. On the day that the movie hit the theaters the stock began to decline. Buy on the rumor and sell on the news proved true.

Caveats

Hot Tips

Hot tips can chill your performance. Seldom do these rush ideas pan out. The person offering the advice is usually not trained to analyze securities and may simply report a conversation he overheard. Playing someone else's hunch is not a recipe for success.

Caveat Emptor

Yes! Let the buyer beware especially with foreign stocks and particularly with Chinese equities. Many of the hyped stocks you hear about in China and in other BRIC countries operate without being under the canopy of protection offered to the investor by the various security laws in the United States.

I own a number of foreign issues but am aware and concerned about problems that can arise from inadequate regulation.

Recognize Environmental Tradeoffs

Déjà vu! The recent oil & gas boom in the Dakota's Bakken Shale formation reminds me of the California gold rush. This is black gold country. In contrast with the rest of the United States, employment is soaring, business is booming and hope abounds.

There is a trade off. In order to unlock the deposits from the shale, a process called "fracking" is used. Unfortunately, it requires a considerable amount of water. It is well known that fresh water supplies are rapidly depleting. One might reasonably expect some fresh government intervention which might raise the costs of the explorations. In addition, there is concern about possible ground water contamination from the extracts.

TERMS YOU SHOULD KNOW

Goodwill

This is an additional value that the company carries as an asset on its books which is more than the sum of its measurable assets. It may come in part as a result of the reputation of the company.

Treasury stock

The company may hold some stock as undistributed. Often this is shares that the board decided to buy back on the open market. It can be used for many corporate purposes including helping to thwart a hostile takeover.

Cash Flow

These measures are indicative of liquidity and positive cash flow is important as a determinant for dividends.

Dead Cat Bounce

I have always loved this hilarious reference to market behavior. It is said that a cat has nine lives perhaps relating to his resiliency in different situations. One phenomenon often cited is that if dropped from any height or position the cat will always land on his feet.

When the market declines for awhile, traders will often say. "We are due for a dead cat bounce." They mean a relief rally is anticipated. It is more colorful to say a dead cat bounce. The basic idea is that even a dead cat will bounce if dropped for any distance.

Macroeconomics

This refers to large units and deals with the overall economy as a whole.

Microeconomics

This term is concerned with the behavior of individual situations. Home economics could be considered a micro concept.

Ladder

This refers to buying investments in successive and possibly increasing increments. You might have a certain amount of money to invest and you want to put it in treasury securities. One way would be to divide the money into parts and buy the current issue, then the next, and the next, etc. I might have treasury strips in 2012, 2015, 2020 and 2030 all bought with a ladder approach. The yield would rise with each increment (normally).

Canary in the coal mine

Coal mines have a sad history of injury and death. This is often caused by a methane gas leak. Miners found that, if they took a canary into the mine and the canary died, it was probable that the level of toxic gas had increased. Then appropriate measures including exit from the mine could be taken. It has since come to be a reference for problems.

PART TWO
MECHANICS

THE STOCK MARKET

I think it was Chaucer who said "Be wise and take the grain but leave the chaff" or something to that effect. This is important because that is what we must do in order to learn the stock market. For the moment, we will set aside an interesting history that led to the development of multiple exchanges such as the NASDAQ, AMERICAN and the NYSE. Let's concentrate on the NYSE, which is called the Big Board. Here most of the big name companies trade such as Caterpillar, DuPont, and General Electric.

One way to gauge the growth of the stock market is to note volume. In the late 1940's, volume was less than a million shares per day. It rapidly grew over the years until today, when normal volume on the New York Stock Exchange is over one billion shares. However, do not be lulled into thinking that all of this is individual volume, on the contrary, much of it is computerized trading by the big institutions and large hedge funds. Comments on that will follow later.

Supply and demand again creeps into the establishment of price. Sellers and buyers compete with each other based upon their interpretation of the relative worth of the stock in the light of supply and demand. You might expect more volatility in price with a "thin" stock, i.e. one that has few shares outstanding as opposed to a stock with many shares available in the marketplace. This is a statistic you need to evaluate in your fundamental considerations.

History does record many abuses in the marketplace in the early years with some legendary characters. Fortunes were made and lost with relative ease because THERE WERE FEW SAFEGUARDS FOR THE PUBLIC. That has changed. Marketplaces are well regulated and the policing of this area falls under the Securities and Exchange Acts of 1933 and 1934. Brokers have guidelines that they must follow and each brokerage house has its own compliance department charged exactly with a mandate to protect the public.

It's Safe Enough Even for a Beginner

Later I will give you personal tips to further protect you in your dealings in the stock market. It can be fun and profitable. Look forward to your first trade.

There is a system called the specialist system which has been of great worth insofar as they are able to facilitate trades. Specialists operate with a book where they match buy and sell orders. If the process reaches an impasse, often the specialist will buy or sell for or from his own account in order to break the deadlock. His role is being diminished by certain computerized processes, but his is a colorful role of fulfillment in market place history.

How Do I Buy a Stock?

You place an order. Notice the stock quote below.

Name	52 week H/L	Vol 100's	Yld	PE	Last trade	Change	Div Amt
ST JOE	27.20 12.72	33,925	----	17	19.23	1.20	---

If you wanted to buy ST JOE paper common stock, you could tell your broker to buy X amount of shares at the market or at a limit price. I will explain more on that later. Change refers to the fact that it was up from the day before. Note that the stock has no dividend so your return must come from price appreciation. You will want to check the candlestick chart to get an idea of its smoothed out movement over a year, and you will want to know the average PE ratio of the market at the time you decide to buy.

You pull up a current quote and note the bid price at 19.0 and the asked price at 19.10. This tells you that a willing buyer would buy at the bid price and a willing seller would sell at the asked or offer price. Then you choose the price you are willing to pay. If the volume per day is low and if there is a wide disparity between the bid and asked prices, I would use a limit order, if not I would simply buy at whatever the market price is at the time.

Now it is time to tame the beast. How do we select a stock (equity) and buy it?

CRITERIA FOR SELECTION
Is the stock solvent?   Is it in the public interest?

Is my choice technically sound?   Is it an investment or a speculation?   Is the chart free of downside gaps?

Is it a brokerage house recommendation or my own choice?

Is my rational for buying growth or income?

What is the dividend policy? Is the dividend covered by earnings?

Is the compensation paid to the officers excessive?

Does the main product appear to have long term viability?

Is it a high beta stock? Is the current ratio normal?

Does it have a product line or is it dependent on a single item?

Let's suppose that you want to buy a railroad stock. Maybe you traced your family back to the heyday of the railroads as I did. So you look in *Barron's* at rail stocks. These are the quotes on your favorite issues.

52 week high	Low	Ave Vol	Yield	PE	change	
Mom's rail	27.20	12.72	33,000	none	19	1.23
Dad's rail	53.10	38.25	66,000	2.0	15	-.50

Next you go check your stocks. You determine both are solvent, obviously in the public eye, both are technically sound, and are considered investments, and neither is a brokerage house recommendation. Your choice comes down to your primary objective. What did you check as your top need on the new account form? Has your need changed? If you are primarily interested in income then Dad's rail is for you. Otherwise the growth choice is best. Incidentally, classical market psychology suggests that for the younger person growth might be a better first choice. For the older person income may have more appeal.

Say you are an income guy and pick Dad's rail. Now what? You have to decide how many shares you want to buy with your $5,000 in available funds. You should have at least four stocks for diversification so you can buy $1250 worth. What is the next selection step? Where will you purchase the stock from, (A) an online broker (B) a full service broker or (C) direct from the company if that service is offered? Dad's rail is now at $54.00 per share so you calculate you can buy 23 shares. Whoa! Can you? You must subtract the probable commission from the available funds and then calculate the number of shares. There are a number of types of stocks available.

Growth stocks

Another name for these might be great expectation companies. That is what you expect from growth stocks. You are looking for stocks with rising earnings and profitability.

Preferred stocks

This is a type of income stock. Don't expect them to act like common stocks. The dividend is the primary appeal as it must be paid before dividends can be paid to common stock holders. Various kinds of preferred stocks are available.

Value stocks

These equities usually have assets that may not be fully valued on the company books. An example might be a company that has land which is carried on the books at cost rather than market value.

Penny Stocks

These are usually very speculative and dangerous. Beware of stocks under $5 per share. These seldom work for the small investor.

Types of Orders

MARKET ORDER. You will get the price at the time the order is executed which is usually within seconds. LIMIT ORDER. You might place an order limit between the bid and the asked hoping to buy it cheaper than the offer price. OPEN ORDER. You pick a price at which you are willing to buy and leave it open for a stated time period.

STOP ORDER. This order tells the broker to buy or sell at a stated price above or below the market. If XUX was 60 and you were afraid it would fall, then you might place a stop order at 56. At 56 it would become a market order and be filled at that or the next price. A stop-limit order is a variation and a stop-limit at 56 would become a limit order and be filled at the limit or better.

I do not like stop or stop limit orders. It seems to me to be an ostrich approach. It is in effect programming a loss. If I think the stock may fall, I prefer an outright sell or use of a covered call.

Shares Outstanding

The number of shares outstanding is quite important as it affects both the buy and sell decision. Too few available shares may mean it is "thin" and bid and asked spreads could be wide, in which case it might be wise to use limit orders instead of market orders.

It would be smart to check to see whether any secondary or shelf issues are planned. If the company floats more stock, your holdings might be diluted and that could change earnings per share. It is a variable you need to consider.

Capitalization

This term refers to the size of the company as small, medium or large cap. Large cap might mean a company with a size of 10 billion, midcap would be 2 to 10 B, and small cap would be below 2B.

Stock splits

Occasionally, a company will split its stock for marketing reasons. A $100 price might be more attractive for buyers at $50 so the company might split two for one. The overall value of your holding would remain the same.

A reverse split usually indicates a serious problem. Here the company might split the stock one for ten. You would surrender your ten shares and receive one share. In my opinion, the real effect of this is to wipe out minority shareholders. The company will put a positive spin on the action but it is seldom a positive event. One stated reason might be to raise the stock price by reducing the outstanding shares such that mutual funds could buy the stock and thus get it out of "penny stock status." Any time a company announces a reverse stock split I run for cover and kick myself for being in such a situation.

Various Markets

NYSE

All listed companies must meet certain listing requirements including the value of their assets, earnings, and number of shares outstanding. The "Big Board" is so called because this is where the majority of household names trade. On a historical note, the New York Stock Exchange was started after daily trading at a place near a tree on Wall Street in 1792. The Exchange was begun at a later date.

AMERICAN

It was sometimes called the "junior exchange". This is where a number of U.S. and Canadian issues trade. Preferred stocks also trade here.

NASDAQ

This is the large market for shares not listed on the NYSE or AMEX. It is sometimes called the OTC market (over the counter). Dealers must be members of the NASD. Early on most issues were quoted in the "pink sheets" which is where many illiquid issues can be found. You can see the NASDAQ market on the ticker directly under the NYSE tape.

REGIONAL   These are smaller exchanges like the Midwest, Philadelphia and Pacific exchanges.

Emerging And Frontier Markets

There does not appear to be a concise list or agreement over the distinction between these two ideas. Emerging markets are in a process of development but have not gotten the distinction of developed markets. These generally involve countries who show gradual improvement and progress in infrastructure, political stability and economics. Now Columbia, Egypt and most BRIC countries are considered emerging markets.

Frontier markets are also emerging but with less progress in infrastructure, political stability and economic change than emerging or developed countries Jamaica and Nigeria would be examples of frontier marketplaces.

Grey Market

I admit that I had not remembered this term from my years as a broker and mention it only as a curiosity. This is a term often used to describe the market that caters to older folks. It is also a market for imported goods obtained legally under unusual conditions such as prior to formal trading for the underlying stock. It is a colorful term but not of real importance to the beginner.

Indicators

These are various economic topics that suggest the health of the economy which has ramifications for the various markets. Professionals tend to favor their own array of indicators. Here are some of many that I consider important.

10-Year Treasury Yield	This is a measure of the bond market

Unemployment Rate	Overall measure of the health of the economy
CPI and PPI	Measures of the cost of goods produced and their prices
Home Sales and Starts	Measure of economic growth
The Factory Utilization Rate	This is a clue to manufacturing activity

You will need to learn to recognize and interpret these kinds of data.

Stock market continued

FORMULAS, INDEXES, BAROMETERS

You cannot learn them all. Don't try. Concentrate on the ones that affect your mind set principles. I will list a few that I follow and consider important.

Current Ratio

This figure is a measure of liquidity. It gives you a quick assessment of the solvency of the company. The formula is as follows: current assets divided by current liabilities equals the current ratio. XYZ has 100,000 in current assets and 80,000 in current liabilities so its current ratio is 1.25. Use this as your base guideline a CR of >1<2.7 is good. Greater than two may indicate that management is not using resources to best advantage or it may reflect an influx of cash.

Copper

Copper (CU). I like to watch the value of copper. Since it is used in so many building applications (including the Statue of Liberty) it serves me as an indicator for the health of the economy. It is found in many places but Chile is considered the biggest producer followed by the United States. It is an excellent conductor of electricity and heat and has a big use in the air conditioning industry. The current price of copper is 3.33 lb.

Rule of 72

Simply stated, it is useful for a quick estimate of how long it would take to double your money. The rule assumes a compounding factor.

Let's say that you have $1,000 dollars to invest and want an estimate of how long it would take to double your money at 6% interest. Just divide the number 72 by 6. It would take 12 years. You can do this mentally as you choose between alternatives as say between a stock and a bond (ignoring the safety factor). It comes in handy in a variety of situations.

PE ratio

This is one of the most important tools you have. The PE ratio numerically relates price and earnings. Price divided by earnings gives you the ratio. If the price is $10 per share and the company is earning 1.00 per share, then the PE ratio is 10. A ratio that is too low in comparison with the DJIA or its own industry average PE is a danger sign, or conversely, an opportunity. Here you must determine why the PE is low and thus you dig further into the financials. A PE ratio that is too high is also of concern. It may reflect an unusual premium given for good performance and enhanced expectations. If it is higher than its competitors then it is even more critical to find out why before you invest.

PE can be even more useful if we solve the equation for price. Suppose that we learn that earnings are supposed to increase by 20%. Our new earnings would be 1.20. Our interest now turns to price. What should the new price be in light of increased earnings? This calculation is imprecise and assumes that the PE stays constant. (PE expansion can take place but usually takes some time so our assumption is safe in the short run). To solve for price, we use this adjusted formula: P='s PE x E or 10 times 1.20. Thus we can expect a move somewhere around 12 with the increase in earnings. Earnings Yield

EPS divided by price equals the earnings yield percentage. It gives you another look at the earning power of a stock. The higher the EY, the more I want to evaluate the fundamentals of the issue. A stock trading at 19.10 with earnings of 1.24 per share would have an earnings yield of 6.49%. It is also the reciprocal of the PE ratio (the same stock had a PE of 15.40 so 1divided by 15.40 equals 6.49%). A low earnings yield or a high PE will suggest that I take another look at the stock before I buy.

Price to Sales

P/S if <1 is considered good especially if it is lower than its competitors. P/S is figured easily by dividing the price per share by the yearly net sales. It is just another metric to examine. Most financial websites will list this figure for you.

Alpha

Alpha is usually used as a measure of mutual fund performance. A high alpha might suggest better than expected performance.

FORMULA FOR DETERMINING THE TRUE WORTH TO YOU BETWEEN A CORPORATE AND A MUNICIPAL BOND

We examine a concept called the Taxable Equivalent Yield. Suppose you are in a 30% tax bracket and need to decide between a 6% corporate bond and a 4.5% municipal bond. For this analysis we assume a safe comparison for safety and relevancy. The equation becomes :

TEY ='s Tax Free Yield divided by 1.0 minus the tax bracket

Or

TEY ='s 4.5 divided by 0.70 (1-.30) or 6.42%

Therefore, from a tax standpoint the 4.5% municipal would seem to be the better buy. This does not allow for any advantage from a state tax standpoint. This is an extremely useful formula.

BOND MARKETS

Bond markets are several and varied. You may decide that you want treasury securities, other government or agency bonds, corporate bonds or municipal bonds. Each of these categories of bonds offers advantages that will satisfy a personal objective. For instance, if you prefer the safest from a secure principle standpoint (ignoring market fluctuations), you might select treasury issues including bills, notes and bonds, which are called marketable securities.

Suppose you want to maximize income that you might choose among the various types of corporate bonds. A desire for tax free income would lead you to municipal bonds and the subdivisions therein. Finally, a high tolerance for risk might bring you to consider the volatile world of high yield bonds.

What you need to know.

Bonds are varied by type and appeal to the investor.

Corporate bonds are issued by a company. Municipal bonds are issued by a city, state, territory or revenue project.

Government bonds and government agency bonds have the appeal of a degree of safety. Zero coupon bonds are bonds that do not pay interest but mature at a stated value at some designated time. Foreign bonds may be bought by the individual investor but have some restrictions and may be best purchased through a mutual fund or ETF that specializes in these bonds.

Zero coupon bonds are sold at a discount from maturity value. An example would be the U.S. government's series E and EE savings bonds but not the I Bond, which is sold at face value and matures with interest. I have successfully used zero coupon bonds as a hedge for my portfolio using a ladder approach of a few at periodic maturity intervals. The volatility allows for a profit if the yields fall, and if not, I have a stated appreciation factor. No income is paid on zeros but the IRS calculates a phantom income component and taxes are paid each year as if that interest was earned that year. Government or agency zeros were also issued but are fast disappearing from the marketplace. These were called Cats and Fico's. Interesting, but these are beyond our scope here.

REMEMBER ONE TRUISM

That price and yield are inversely related

If interest rates go up, bond prices always fall. If interest rates go down then bond prices go up (assuming all else is constant).

So if you hear someone say, "Yields on treasuries went up" you would know that the price of treasury bonds had fallen. Conversely, if someone said, that "Prices on municipals went north today.", you would know that municipal bond prices went up, thus the yields went down.

THIS IS INCREDIBALY VALUABLE INFORMATON NEVER FORGET IT IF YOU BUY ANY FIXED INCOME PRODUCT

Bonds have ratings given to them by so called "rating agencies" and range from AAA to default. Recently, the U.S. government had its overall rating lowered for the first time in history. Isn't that scary? Also, at this time foreign governments had strains on their debt. Greece was recently lowered to C, which is an extremely low rating and suggests they will be unable to meet their obligations.

Municipals

These are very attractive for investors who need tax advantaged income. Municipals (muni's) are issued by cities and states to pay for necessary projects in infrastructure, schools, bridges, medical , etc. Usually, you will need to choose between a revenue bond or a general obligation bond. In the formula section, I gave you a formula to help you determine whether a municipal or a corporate bond would be better for you.

The bond will have a coupon yield which may or not be the actual yield to you. Yield to call and yield to maturity are very important concepts. Just know that if the yield to maturity is greater than the coupon yield the bond will be priced at a discount from its stated value. If you have a call feature on the bond which allows the company to retire it before its maturity date, then your actual yield may be lower than the coupon yield.

You may see these terms when you get your confirmation. If it says that the dealer acted as an agent, then he charged a commission and this is known as a markdown. If he acts as a principal, then he trades from his own inventory and this will be noted as a markup.

Corporate bonds

One advantage of bonds is that they sell for price plus accrued interest. So if I buy a bond from X I will pay whatever the bond sells for plus accrued interest to the date of the sale. I will get the full amount of the interest when paid, but I am compensating the seller for his hold of the bond up to the date of sale. This is an advantage over selling a dividend stock because if the seller sells in advance of the X date of the distribution then he loses his right to the next dividend payment.

A corporate bond is quoted in terms of a % of value. A bond selling at 98 5/8 is priced at $986.25 per bond. Normally you will buy in a lot of at least 5 bonds. Later you will need to learn the differences in how yields are quoted i.e. Yield to maturity, yield to call, nominal yield, etc. Corporate bonds are rated with the highest rating being AAA or Aaa. Those above BBB are considered investment grade. Remember, if you step down a notch in rating to pick up additional yield, you will also increase your risk. Be sure to check the fundamentals of the underlying company (current ratio, long term debt to equity ratio, industry position, etc) before you chase additional yield. I believe any bonds rated below BBB are best left to investment professionals through mutual funds.

REMEMBER THE SECOND TRUISM
INFLATION OR DEFLATIONARY EXPECTATIONS
MOVE VALUES ON BONDS

Our old friend economics surfaces again. Inflation or deflation, or the expectation thereof, will cause bonds prices to move.

An expectation of inflation will cause price to fall.

An expectation of deflation will cause price to rise (but bondholders may find their stream of income interrupted if debtors are unable to pay).

This subject alone could necessitate an entire book for complete understanding but as this is a primer we will move forward. I will offer these points with respect to buying bonds.

1. Don't buy from the so called two point or scrap inventory list. Your broker can explain. These are individual pieces which may involve big commissions and be hard to resell. I always buy a bond in at least a five bond lot (5,000 face).

2. Choose the bond that fits your taxable need status. See the formula section for an idea on how to choose.

3. Avoid municipal bonds that carry AMT (alternative minimum tax).

4. Consider the use of zero coupon bonds as a hedge but understand the high volatility associated with this investment (look to use these when you do not expect high inflation.)

Yield Curve

The yield curve is a picture of the relationship between interest and time. The longer the time frame, the more yield you should expect for the added risk. An upward slopping yield curve is normal. The flatter the yield curve the less growth is expected. An inverted yield curve would be one where shorter maturities yield more than longer maturities. I suggest you try to learn more about the nature of the yield curve especially as it behaves in stressful times.

THE SWEAT OF THE SUN

Early on in my career as a broker I gained an appreciation for precious metals as a foundation for a portfolio and gave lectures in the 1980's on the subject. I also went to an old mining town and actually panned for gold. It was hard work and my back hurt for days. I realize that primitive people still use this procedure in such places as South America, the Pacific Rim and Africa. Now is a historically high price range for gold and in frontier and emerging markets without real mining technology it is a safe bet that poor people will still sift the soil. Placer also called surface or open pit mining as was done in the old days of the gold rush at Sutter's Mill in California is difficult work. Meteorites were recently found there. I believe it was the Inca's who called gold, "The sweat of the sun."

I was often called on locally for my knowledge of these markets when gold was just beginning its climb. At that time, the big secret was the incredible dividend yields of the gold miners especially in South Africa. Gold deposits there were found in concentrated areas called reefs. These were formed when seas in the region cooled and gold was deposited as the sea receded. Today much of the easily found gold has been mined and new hazards abound. Mines are often several miles deep. Costs have risen and there have been changes in the political area as well.

Of course, there are other producing regions even in the U.S., Canada, Russia, Mexico, South America and especially Brazil. All are producers, as are some countries along the Pacific Rim. Each of these countries have mining problems to content with as in Canada where it can be the extreme cold and permafrost conditions that interrupt mining.

Our old friends demand and supply rule these markets. Some demand is seasonal. Christmas is such an occasion. Jewelry use is a big demand factor. In India it is customary for brides to wear their gold dowry around the neck. Central bankers try to hedge their portfolios with some precious metal anchor (as you should do). In general, since the heyday of easy gold finds, supply tends to be tighter than when I first recommended gold and silver.

I used this argument which was standard fare in the literature and is still used today. It is known as the uniform argument. I would ask, "What would a Roman centurion, a Revolutionary soldier and a U.S. Marine have in common in any time considered?" The answer was and still is that an ounce of gold would buy a fine uniform in every case. Idea here is that gold retains its value.

Then I would continue with the main reasons to buy gold which are:

1. As a medium of exchange   2. As a store of value

3. As a hedge against inflation.   4. As portfolio insurance.

Then I would ask what countries in the world had known serious inflation. Some would say the Roman Empire (emperors would shave down their coins so that the true worth was lessened but eventually the populace caught on to it), others would suggest France and Germany and both were correct (Germanys hyperinflation of 1923 is often remarked as a lesson point as was the Assignats in France but I never got an answer from a client about the U.S.. The U.S. had its currency wiped out twice with the continental dollar and the greenback of the Civil War. And our own dollar has lost value. Most recently Zimbabwe's inflation is a recent standout.

Gold has held its value. When people no longer trust their currency they will turn to gold. Now it seems that we have another reason to buy gold # 5 as currency (similar to #1). In a barter type of economy, small gold coins will satisfy almost any necessity.

We need to move on but I would pick number three as the primary reason for owning gold. Inflation destroys the purchasing power of currencies. There is ample history to support this statement. Don't overload your portfolio but consider at least a five percent holding in precious metals.

Gold has an interesting modern history. Early in our nations monetary history both gold and silver served as monetary standards (bi-metallic backed currency). The Gold Standard Act came in 1900 and made our currency backed by gold. In 1933 private ownership of gold was outlawed by President Roosevelt. For a long time gold had an official price of $35 per ounce. In 1971 president Nixon closed the gold window which eliminated the gold standard i.e. our currency backed by gold. At this time, no currency in the world is totally backed by a precious metal. Nixon had to act as most of our currencies gold reserves held at Fort Knox were being paid out to settle international debts. Keep your eye on the government official price of gold as it changes. There have been legal cases where gold was lost in transit and it was settled by the official government price which, of course, was much below the market price.

Question: How much gold should I have in a barter situation?

The best answer to this that I have heard is I believe attributed to a NYSE floor broker, who said,

"You should have enough to bribe the guard at the border."

This comment implies two situations. First, that if you were in that situation you would be satisfying one of the prime reasons to own gold and you would certainly be in a chaotic marketplace. Second, the broker meant that in the most extreme of cases gold (or silver) would work as a tradable substitute currency.

The Amazonian Rain Forrest is being ravaged by illegal placer mine operations. The primitive use of mercury is polluting both the soil and water. Sometimes the quest for profit especially by the uninformed brings on horrible consequences.

What about Silver?

It is often called the poor man's gold. Silver is unique in that it has some precious metal allure but it is primarily an industrial metal. Yet, the reasons to own gold are good for silver as

for numismatic items. They are fun to collect and can be profitable. If you should travel abroad especially in South America, and some vendor offers you a seemingly old coin perhaps in the early 1700's, be careful as it may not be valuable. It is a policy in some countries to restrike old coins and carry the original mint date. You could be easily tricked.

OTHER COMMODITY MARKETS

Basic commodities such as lead, copper, iron, etc are best invested though the futures markets. I will add that in my opinion the most important one to watch is copper. Its uses are many and often a move here will signal a move in the market. I would as a beginner learn to watch the price of copper as one indicator for timing of purchase or sell decisions.

What about platinum?

Primary sources are South Africa and Russia. There is much less of it in the U.S. but one minable source was found in Montana. It is one of the so called white metals (platinum group) and because of its resistance to corrosion it is also called a Noble metal. It is used in car assemblies, especially in catalytic convertors and spark plugs. It has also been used in the new Fuel Cell applications. And it has electrical uses as it is also strongly non-reactive. It is a very rare metal much more so than gold or silver. Like gold and silver, platinum coins are sold. Today a one ounce $100 platinum bullion coin would sell for about $1,787 which includes the dealer markup. Seldom has platinum sold at a discount to gold but recently it did. That relationship may offer opportunity to the astute precious metals investor.

BASE METALS

These are not in our scope here but some familiarity with these is recommended. Tin, lead, antimony, and titanium are all important and interesting. Titanium is used in many applications such as paint and most especially in airplanes. Prices of these may not be as volatile as the precious metals but available supply is the key to price.

RARE EARTH METALS

This is a group of seventeen metals such as Yttrium and Cerium, which are used in a lot of specialized applications including metallurgical, electronic and petroleum based uses. Much of the known supply of REM's is in China. It is an area of future focus. Not all are exceedingly rare except perhaps in volumes of mineable ore. A recent interesting use is in the circuitry of cell phones.

PERSONAL INVESTMENT POINTERS

All of these don'ts should be considered to be prefaced by "in my opinion." Almost any of my comments in this list would elicit serious rebuttal from those who sell the product or provide the service. I strongly believe in these caveats based upon my personal experience.

- Never sign discretionary account papers.
- Never list speculation as an objective on the New Account Form unless it is 100% your objective.
- Never follow a broker who has habitual compliance issues.
- Never place an annuity in an IRA.

- Never leave personal financial information in an open area that is not protected by you or your broker. Guard against identity theft.
- Never brag about your success or failure. Remember, mum's the word.
- Never fail to be diversified. In mutual funds that includes allocation across companies and across managers.
- Never sell precious metals to an outfit by mail.
- Never trade on a tip. Trade only on your research finding.
- Never sell short if you can use a simple option technique as a hedge. In addition I seldom use any option technique other than covered calls. I do not favor the use of margin for a beginner.
- Never ignore the potential risks of commodity trading and do not forget that you will be hampered in trading by less than instantaneous access to distant factors that affect trading (such as droughts, earthquakes, tidal waves, cyclones or deforestation) where by the time you get the information it may have been largely acted upon.
- Never forget that if you are an active trader you should ask for and receive a discounted fee.

OTHER PRODUCTS AND OTHER MARKETS

CD'S

Not a bad choice necessarily but perhaps not a best choice. Here you are absolutely exposed to reinvestment risk. If you have a 6% CD now, you may not get a 6% return when it matures. As a bedrock investment some certificates of deposit might be advisable (fall back security). Just don't overload with this investment.

MUTUAL FUNDS

This is an investment company product which envelopes certain investments such as stock and bonds. Investors pick a mutual fund which matches their objective of growth, income, value or some mixture of these. Mutual funds are professionally managed and each investor buys shares in the fund itself not in the components of the fund. These funds offer liquidity, diversification, and professional management. The funds are regulated by the U.S. Securities and Exchange

Commission (SEC). Each fund must provide a prospectus to the investor. These are designed as long range investment vehicles. The investor can choose from several thousand available issues.

Mutual funds are products issued with an established portfolio of stocks or bonds or some combination thereof. This is a great starter product for young investors. They offer diversification and liquidity. The funds stand ready to buy or sell shares on a daily basis. Since there are thousands of choices you must select wisely.

The first step is to remind yourself of your objective whether it be growth, income or value. Then find a fund in that area with a good track record and an established manger. Here is a mutual fund quote.

	Nav	Offer	% change
CXYZA	10.90	11.23	-.04

NAV is the Net Asset Value per share which is calculated daily. Next is the offer price and the third column shows the change from the previous day. So if you buy your fund you would pay 11.23 per share, if the price is the same the next day because net asset value is calculated at the close of each trading day.

Some points to consider:

1. See how long the manager has been at the helm. (Better if he has been aboard awhile.)

2. See what the funds asset base is because a real small capitalization could be a major problem in a selloff.

I would be very worried if my fund was less than 100 million minimum.

3. Check the performance of the fund (by its type) i.e. do not look for growth percentages in a bond fund. Look to see if the fund matched or beat the industry average for that type of fund. Also, look at the alpha.

Prospectus

Mutual funds are required by law to send you a prospectus soon after the purchase. This document will outline the purpose of the fund, costs, probable risks and more. It should be read by the investor.

UIT'S

Unit Investment Trusts are packaged investments offered by a brokerage house which usually has a fixed portfolio. The markets for these are largely thin. I do not favor these unmanaged funds. It is a matter of personal choice and I prefer mutual funds. I consider these rather static investments.

ETF'S

Here is a sample ETF (closed end fund) quote.

Nav	Price	Prem/disc	52 week return
13.90	12.57	-9.6	11.2

ETF's are exchange traded funds that hold a select basket of securities. I favor these for having participation in a particular country. This way I can customize my exposure to that countries risk. The fund usually holds a basket of their best securities. One big plus to this purchase is the fact that most have very low expense ratios (annual fee based upon assets.) Be careful of these funds that have very small asset bases. Often they are designed to track an index although seldom perfectly perform as designed.

There are tax events to consider when owing ETF'S, especially commodity type situations such as gold and silver products. These can be considered collectibles subject to higher capital gains taxes. Also, K-1 tax reporting can be involved in some specialized types. This does not diminish the overall attractiveness of this type of investment in unique applications.

MLP'S

Income is passed through a partnership structure. These are subject to government regulation risk. Many of these are in the energy area. Keep in mind that oil and gas extraction involves depletion of the asset. Even in 2012 there is still talk about the question of "peak oil" and the great expectation that the various shale formations will make up the short fall. Also with MLP's there can be some tax issues. I understand the high dividend opportunity but I am not enamored by this vehicle.

TARGET FUNDS

Most mutual fund companies now offer so called target funds which are designed to maximize value as of particular designated date such as a target fund due in 2035. The idea is sound enough in theory but in practice, not so much.

First, it assumes that you do not have the expertise to pick investments for yourself and further the assumption is that your objective would be identical with the fund manager over that time frame. Seldom is that the case.

The fund itself may offer a low expense ratio (smoke screen, in my opinion). It is the diversification that is suspect. Many of the funds invest the portfolio entirely within their own in house funds. I looked at two different no load funds as I was writing this excerpt. Both funds were identical in that there was not a single blue chip stock or individual bond. Instead in each case the portfolio was 90% or more of that companies funds. Where is the diversification? The manager will carry the overall in house bias toward the market direction and who can predict that reliably over many years in the future?

It is not the return so much that bothers me as the egotistical nature of the fund managers' bias, i.e. any of our funds are better choices for you than a competitors might be. I believe that a selected laddered program of zero coupon bonds together with a few blue chip stocks adjusted as you invest might give a better overall return.

When I encounter such a bias, whether a part of the structure of the investment or not, I run for cover. Perhaps you should as well.

ANNUITIES

There are three types: fixed, variable and immediate. Basically, you give the company x dollars for y time and they pay you z for interest. This is an example of a tax deferred product. Earnings are deferred but not normally tax free. I am not friendly to this product for several reasons. There can be a number of fees including one called a surrender fee which may last for a number of years. One particular caveat is that it can be a high commission product for the selling broker. Be sure you understand this product thoroughly before you even contemplate its purchase. The death benefit is touted as the major advantage.

Futures Markets

Futures (commodity contract trading)

Not for the beginner. These markets can be treacherous. I tell you to stay away even though I actually traded futures. I came quickly to the realization that I would not be successful in this arena.

The futures markets are quick to move on new information. If you do not have nearly instantaneous access to these new facts that the traders will have in the major marketplaces of the world then you will fail. For example, let's say that there is a coffee crop failure in Brazil and you hear about it 24 hours later. Most often the coffee market will have absorbed the news before you can react.

What are futures? Usually we think of commodities such as grains, metals, livestock, currencies, lumber etc. If you are a beginner how will you choose among these broad areas? Suppose you decide to invest in the grain markets then which grain, corn, wheat, oats, rapeseed, should you choose? And if you invest you must know the relationships between the grains. Same goes for metals, lumber, livestock, coal and the rest.

What would you do if you had to take delivery of a commodity? It's not a joke, you could find yourself owning the physical item itself. How about taking delivery of 110,000 board feet of lumber? Leave futures alone for now. However, let me tell you there are great commodity traders but they are very dedicated and have the capital necessary to absorb what could be major losses.

OPTIONS TRADING

Talk about some colorful terms. Alligator spread (jokingly), put-call spread, covered calls, calendar spreads and more. This area is also very dangerous and best left for a time when you are experienced. I have traded options on many occasions but now for simplicity I limit myself to writing covered calls. This will be suitable for you when you have some real experience in buying and selling equities.

The basic idea in options is to utilitize time to your advantage. An option in the stock market is like an option in other places. You operate within a time frame where there is a decay factor. Let's look at a simple covered call. You own 100 shares of XYZ Company. You have a profit and think the stock may go down from the current price of 50 so you are willing to sell it to someone else who has the opposite opinion. You might be willing to sell a 55 call for $1. The other party may buy the option and pay you $1. So your sell price would be 56 on the stock that you think may go down.

What happens next? If the stock goes to 57 in the time frame allowed, the other party will likely exercise the option and pay you 55 per share. The $100 you earned from selling the option is yours. If the stock goes down below 55 in the time frame, you keep the stock and if the option expires worthless you have earned an extra $100. Properly used, this technique is often profitable.

To use a covered call, you must own 100 shares of the stock.

If you engage in any form of option trading, you will be sent the booklet called "Characteristics and Risks of Standardized Options" as well as any recent supplements. You should examine this booklet carefully.

HOMEWORK ASSIGNMENT

Imagine how the markets are affected by landmark events

LANDMARKS

Technology Wreck of 2000	Debt disaster of 1998	Asian Crisis of 2007
Energy crisis of the 1970's	Real Estate Investment Trust bust of 1974	
Bond market decline of 79-80	Banking and Savings & Loan 1980's crisis	
Twin Tower Terrorism	Lehman Brothers collapse	Great Recession of 09-10
Sovereign debt implosion in Europe in 11-12,	Lowering of U.S. debt rating	
Arab Spring riots	(Egypt, Syria etc ongoing in 12),	Tokyo nuclear meltdown
Crash of 1987	Municipal bond defaults in California and Alabama & elsewhere.	
Dot- Com bubble of 1999.		

It can be useful to see how events disrupt the markets.

The above are some notable reference points. Get a graph of the DJIA and see how these events roiled the markets.

SUMMARY

Global Considerations

As I look back upon my career in the investment business some facts are inescapable now that were not as apparent when I started. The world is in flux and all of it matters. I can remember when problems in Thailand caused market shifts that were most unexpected. Today the world is in turmoil from wars but also from a simple lesson in economics, which is if you outspend your income, trouble follows. More than at any other time I can remember that is the case with sovereign governments. Much of Europe is in financial crisis; that may have begun with Greece but has spread like wildfire. Many countries in Europe are deeply in debt and will need to be rescued by stronger nations.

We also are deeply in debt and our national currency has lost much of its value. While politicians wrestle with improbable answers, ordinary folks (unprepared to face serious economic problems) suffer. Foreclosures are near or at a record. Learn common sense economics-- that is my message to you. It might be nice to know about indifference curves, efficient market theories, misery indexes and other peripheral economic subjects but what you must know is what will affect your investments.

POINT: Global Economic Problems must be a focal point for you.

It almost seems as if countries, like companies, ascend to greatness, plateau, and then wane. An example might be Japan, which became a big economic power after the war years then declined. Of course, the ancient stories of the Greek, Mayan and Roman city states are well known and after that the rise and fall of Germany among others. Most recently, Zimbabwe has the worse inflation on record. Imagine a 100 trillion dollar bill being worth only a few cents.

Well, what now? The past is a historical curiosity, the present an indicator of trend, but the future if you can envision it, is where the riches lie. I would echo what many have been saying: the countries of Brazil, India, China, and to some extent even Russia in its current splintered form and Africa will be the world powers.

Of course, the other great is the United States. Yet there are alarming similarities to other fallen economic powers. Militarily we still are the superpower but we may be losing that economic distinction. Recently, our debt rating was lowered from AAA. This was unimaginable in my boyhood or even a few years ago. It is a direct result of excessive spending and an unfavorable trade imbalance which has led to a punishing decline in our currency. And the constant bickering between the two main political powers has made us seem pitiable in the world's estimation.

China is the real threat now. We have borrowed so much from them and Japan to finance our spending programs that the value of their U.S. debt holdings (Treasury bonds) falls almost daily. They are already looking for an escape hatch—remember my comments on having an escape plan. Quietly they are stockpiling large quantities of commodities such as gold, silver and copper even base materials. They have active acquisition programs in the underdeveloped emerging and frontier nations of the world. We and they have an economic tie in that we are their largest trading partner so overt punitive actions will appeal to them less than will destruction by stealth. Look out for China. Currently, they are proposing a move away from the dollar as the world's reserve currency and they are slowly diversifying away from their purchases of our bonds.

Who is the up and comer? In my opinion, Africa is the power of the future. It has abundant and varied resources, cheap labor, vast land areas and a populace with an increasing capitalistic appetite. Yes, there are pirates, tribal disputes, impossible political situations and incredible poverty. I had already invested in several African issues before the front page article in *Barron's* in 2011 which pointed out the attractiveness for investment. However, issues may be thin. Be careful. A mutual fund or an ETF might be a good starting point for a foray into Africa.

CHARTING

Just a short revisit

Charts reflect the struggle between supply and demand and the implied equilibrium point where they balance to represent a fair price. The technician believes that all that is known about a stock will be reflected in its price. Most commodities trade this way as well.

A great investor once said "The trend is your friend", another said, "Don't fight the tape." The idea behind both prescient statements is that if you watch the trend develop you will be quick to notice changes in sentiment.

Look for gaps in the chart for clues as to where the trend will head. Another useful maxim is that "All gaps are filled." A chart gap below the current price would give me cause for concern and I would be more comfortable with a gap above the current price. It will be useful for you to familiarize yourself with certain types of patterns such as head and shoulders, saucer bottoms, flags, pendants, and reversal and continuation patterns.

Some working knowledge of technical analysis can make you a better investor. Try it; its fun to know. It might also be useful to learn the statistical normal distribution pattern called a Bell curve.

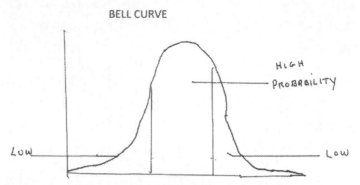

The curve suggests that the majority of data tends to fall toward the center of the graph. I only mention this curve because I believe it is helpful to picture in your mind how cumulative data might be arrayed.

The considerable mathematics behind the curve is not important to us but the idea that data outside of an expected range (said to be skewed) is useful. This might be of importance in analyzing long term financial data. However in truth this is not an idea that most brokers incorporate into their decision making.

If you see data that is wildly erratic in the financials of the company, try arranging it into a bell curve pattern. You may find something of interest.

Bell curve

It is a curve based on the probability of data distribution.

Candlestick chart

Another point to be considered is whether the chart suggests a continuation pattern or a reversal pattern. We could look at all the various configurations of trend such as head and shoulders, island reversals, saucer bottoms, flags, pennants and such but all this can come with experience. The purpose of the chart in its simplest form is to give you some idea of the sentiment behind the issue. A chart is like a famous painting: the more you understand the painter's intent the more valuable will it be to you and the more perspective you will gain. That is the gist of charting.

Two important concepts to consider in the chart are support and resistance. I have drawn these lines for you. If a stock breaks through its resistance line, that point becomes the new support line. Support reflects the area at which a stock has paused or bounced off and resumed the uptrend. Resistance is the ceiling that marks the last advance of the stock. The points on these imaginary lines suggest buy and sell decisions.

DOJI CANDLESTICK IMAGES

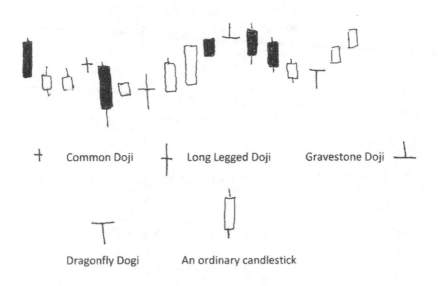

+   Common Doji   ┼   Long Legged Doji   Gravestone Doji ⊥

Dragonfly Dogi   An ordinary candlestick

I favor candlestick charts and these are some of the signs I particularly pay attention to as indications of continuation or reversal patterns. The Dogi often is suggestive of indecision. The ordinary candlestick is composed or a real body and a shadow.

Candlestick chart

XYZ AND AYK
An exercise

For this exercise you will need two pieces of paper or index cards. On the first piece write XYZ and on the other write AYK. On the following page I will list numerous facts and figures which could be a description for either company. If you think that the item mentioned is good put it on the XYZ page and if bad then write it on the AYK page. When finished check your results against mine. All the good points would be arguments for selecting XYX as an equity purchase and the bad points would argue against the AYK selection. This is a way for you to learn how to evaluate whether to buy or sell equity. Each item is different.

Here are the selection points to consider

The company has 18 employees The company has 10,000 employees

The company directors include six people with the same last name

The highest paid director is paid 1.5 million and the next officer is paid $800,000

The current ratio for the company is less than one

The company beta for the company with a current ratio of less than one is 2

Revenues have been increasing for the last 10 years. Dividend growth has been excellent with dividends increased each year for the last ten.

The product line has many items.   The largest buyer is the U.S. government

The chief officer is paid 10 million dollars per year with large stock options

There have been no insider purchases in two years other than exercised stock grants.

The company has used up its revolving line of credit

The company has over 50% of its long term debt coming due within two years.

The current ratio is 1.9

Candlestick chart pattern shows a long term gradual uptrend.

Candlestick pattern is erratic with a large downside gap on the chart

Average age of the directors is 64 and two are older than 70

Most of the officers have degrees and reflect a cross-section of the country

Many well known mutual funds own the stock

Your brother-in-law is a director of the company

Class action lawsuits alleging misrepresentation have been filed against a director

Patent protection on its flagship product will expire next year.

XYZ COMPANY

The company has 10,000 employees. The product line has many items.

The current ratio is 1.9

Revenues have been increasing for the last ten years with dividend growth.

Candlestick chart pattern is favorable.

The 1.5 million salary is not terribly unusual for a successful officer.

Many well known mutual funds owns the stock

Most of the officers have degrees and reflect the U.S. as a whole rather than a particular region.

Many well known mutual funds own the stock (in strong hands)

Conclusion

Not really enough information to make a decision but the initial glance is favorable.

AYK COMPANY

The company has over 50% of its long term debt due within two years.

(Not good, indicates potential bind)

The company has 18 employees.

Maybe a start up, venture capital company (initial risk)

The company has used up its revolving line of credit.

(Limit on borrowing may hinder production.)

The largest buyer is the U.S. government.

(Any buyer with majority of orders can be a problem.)

(Especially the U.S. government with changing policies)

The chief officer is paid 10 million dollars per year and gets options.

(Is he really worth that much? Check the annual returns.)

No insider purchases except exercised stock options.

(If the company insiders aren't buying, should you?)

The current ratio for the company is less than one.

(Trouble! This indicates a possible solvency problem.)

Patent protection will run out next year.

Six AYK directors have the same last name. Lawsuits are not good.

(Tendency to a single management focus-less innovation perhaps)

Beta of 2 with a low current ratio can be a problem (volatility & instability)

Candlestick pattern is erratic with a large downside gap on the chart.

Conclusion

Average age of the directors is troubling. No younger talent. Note the possibility of conflict of interest (insider problems) with a relative on the board.

Now you can see how to organize your thoughts about a company. If you follow this example, you should make better decisions. I would like to know more about AYK but my impression at this point would be not to buy. Remember to use both fundamental and technical analysis to form an opinion.

Selecting a broker

Well, now you are prepared with a mastery of a few sound guidelines that I wanted you to have as a beginner. You are finally ready to make the first really important choice of your investment career. Get help or do it yourself.

You may attempt to do your own thing online or with mutual funds or with direct company purchases (much smaller universe of choices as some companies to not allow direct investments) or you may decide to hire a broker. How do you proceed? More importantly, how can you make a character judgment on someone you have never met? Finally, what qualities should your assistant, mentor, guide (for he is all of that) have?

If I were making this selection, I would want a broker who is like a boy scout. That is, he or she follows the tenets of the Boy Scout Oath. Most important of these is TRUSTWORTHY. He must be that or he will hurt you. Fortunately, due to brokerage house departments called compliance, the broker will usually walk a tight legal line.

Here is what I would want in my first broker. In my first meeting, I would try to probe for as many of the Boy Scout traits as possible. Ask questions. You are entitled to do so and he should expect it. Additionally, I want a broker who is in his late 20's or 30's with at least five years experience as a broker. A investment professional in his 50's or 60's will have an established clientele and be thinking of his retirement which is not a prescription for his giving you his undivided attention. He will instead be devoted to his long term clients.

I must have a broker who selects his own investments and does not simply use the company approved list or be enslaved by the archaic prudent man rule.

I will probe for his opinion on options. If he is too quick to favor options, I don't want him unless his bent is toward covered calls which is the least dangerous option method and one that can be profitable when properly used.

I do not want a broker who likes to short stocks. Short selling is very risky. Postpone this until you are experienced or never do it. Yes, markets do go down and yes, betting on the downside can be profitable, but they also go up and that is where short selling can eviscerate you. Leave it alone.

Finally, and this is paramount, the broker must be trained in and use technical analysis. Preferably, he should have a favorable bent toward Candlestick charting which is my favorite method. Otherwise, he may see the glass half full. Failure to use a technical analysis method (be it point and figure, bar or line chart or candlesticks) dooms my relationship with him.

Also, I want a broker who recommends all investments i.e. stocks, bonds, mutual funds, ETF's, etc. That shows his investment prowess. Further, all investments have a niche and a time—a time for value, for income, for growth even for cash.

Ask questions in an attempt to know your broker.

- Where do you think the stock market is headed in the next few months?
- What do you think of technical analysis? Is there a chart pattern you prefer?
- How should I allocate my resources now? How much in stocks, bonds etc? (This is called asset allocation.)
- How long have you been a broker? How many firms have you worked at?
- Have you ever been in an arbitration hearing? He will not like this question but it is a fair question. He should answer no, if he answers yes, ask why? I will be satisfied with an answer that indicates he was drawn into the situation. Branch managers may wind up in arbitration proceedings that do not reflect something that they have done wrong.
- What is your favorite option technique? If he says anything other than covered calls, either find another broker or make it clear to him that you are an investor and not a speculator.

AND NOW THE MOST IMPORTANT POINT

Do not walk in, sit down and say I have x dollars to invest. He will be quick to figure a way to utilize those funds. Instead say something like; "I would like to begin a gradual, small program with say, x dollars." Then add, "Do you mind working with a small amount to begin our relationship?" Hesitation here would be a negative. If he doesn't want the small investor, he will not want you. If you tell him you are wealthy, he will see dollar signs.

NEXT MOST IMPORTANT POINT

Do not sign Discretionary Authority papers

Discretionary authority allows your broker to buy and sell what he wants, when he wants. If you have a bad broker, in my opinion, this is a recipe for disaster. NEVER sign away your right (and I might add your obligation to yourself) to participate in the buy-sell decision, especially if you checked speculation on the New Account Form. Hopefully you listened to me in my preceding comments on risk. I am against this because it lessens your need to learn the mechanics.

Trust yourself

Who better? You have two basic choices in the investment game. Make the decisions yourself or trust a surrogate. If you delegate to someone else, you will assume this:

1. They have the same mind-set principles that you hold.

2. They will be good stewards of your funds.

3. They are experts or at least as well trained as you expect they are.

Yes, you will need someone to execute your orders. I suggest you will be more likely to succeed if the orders originate with you. Learn what I have tried to teach you and learn from your mistakes. Also, learn to use investment web-sites and periodicals which deal with investments. Be diversified. Start with the idea that no single investment should be more than 5% of your available funds. Trust yourself!

Let me share a personal note on broker training with you. Shortly after I had been hired as a broker, I was sent to New York to study for the insurance, commodities and securities license tests. I was there for several weeks of intensive study. I passed the exams and came home eager to begin.

On my first day at the office, I was given a cubicle and a cold call list with instructions on how to solicit clients by telephone. At the end of the day, my branch manager came up to me and said, "I want you to go meet Mr. X." I asked, why?

He replied, "Because he is a seasoned broker who can give you some insights on how to shortcut your learning curve." I went to the Blue Mood bar in search of Mr. X who liked to go there after hours with some of his clients. He was sitting at the bar and was eating a large seafood dinner.

"You the kid I am supposed to wet nurse?" he asked.

I answered, "Yes."

"Well, I ain't got time but I promised the Branch Manager I would talk to you so what do you want to know?"

"Tell me how to be a good broker."

"Good brokers come and go in this business by the dozens. Only smart brokers survive. Only two things you have to know to become a smart broker."

"Tell me, please."

He continued. "Never forget this, the customer is king. To keep him you cannot treat him as a profit center."

I said that I didn't understand.

"Don't treat him only as a source of your income. Instead, treat him as a family member. Nurture him, watch out for him and follow the physicians lead."

"Which is?"

"First, do no harm. And the second thing to know is always keep some powder dry. Keep some funds in reserve and that way you can take advantage of another opportunity. In summary, treat him as a family member and guard his funds and you will survive. Now get lost, I'm busy."

Mr. X wasn't the friendliest guy in the world but he was a smart broker and I will never forget his cautions. I practiced them my entire career, and I did survive in what I consider to be the toughest business on earth.

I wrote a short story about an old broker who taught a young broker the ropes. It is an intriguing and realistic portrait of the mind set of brokers. You can find this story in my book *Existential Musing* of a *Southern Individualist* which was also published by iUniverse. If this investment primer piques your interest in the market, I know you will enjoy reading this short story. Why not order a copy of the book and read about Renaissance Man and his young protégé.

The Nature of Debt

In a strange way, debt might be considered a cornerstone of growth. People and governments borrow to finance projects and lifestyles which may in turn foster further projects in a domino fashion. Governments take on debt ostensibly to provide services. I cannot imagine an economy where it is not useful.

Yet, misused debt can bring down the borrower. Understanding the nature of debt is an essential step to becoming independent. These days a personal profile will naturally include a debt profile such as a credit rating or financial statement.

Let's see how debt can be useful to governments. For illustration, suppose for the moment that a tiny country, say Garard, owes one million dollars to a larger county called Plume. When would it be a good time for Garard to make a payment on the debt? First, remember our discussion on inflation and deflation and the effect on bonds. In inflation you would rather be a debtor as you are paying down your debt in currency that is worth less (unless the debt is tied to an escalation index but in constant terms this is true). So tiny country Garard owns a million dollars and sees the value of its currency fall from one dollar in constant value to fifty cents on the dollar.

If at this time, Garrard makes full payment, the country will pay its debt (still owning one million dollars) in half for a saving of $500,000. Thus remember this important point.

GIVEN A NECESSARY POLICY CHOICE BETWEEN INFLATION AND DEFLATION GOVERNMENTS WILL ALMOST ALWAYS CHOOSE INFLATION.

A FINAL WORD

I have tried to introduce certain concepts which will make you a better investor. Let me summarize some of the important points.

1. Supply and demand are the most critical concepts to embrace. Rethink the guns and butter allocation problem that is taught in most first level economic courses. Asset allocation is a similar concept you apportion your assets to coincide with your objectives and with prudence.

2. Remember the concept of money as a commodity. Too much money may cause a loss of purchasing power and that is the dollar's problem today. Printing presses alleviate problems, but they do not solve them. That is evident in the hyperinflation stories of Germany, France, Zimbabwe and possibly to come of the U.S as well.

3. Also remember the concept of "ALL DEBT IS PAID". This prescient statement was told to me by a mutual fund manager over dinner. It is true. Debt is satisfied by the debtor repaying the debt or by a reduction in net worth of the creditor.

4. Learn to think in terms of Opportunity Cost. What is the value of the alternative you did not

select? On retrospect, was it a better choice? This is how you learn to evaluate situations.

5. Perhaps most important of all is the concept of the glass half full. You must use both fundamental and technical analysis in order to make reasoned choices for investment.

6. Above all, be diversified. Your financial preservation depends upon this simple fact.

7. Remember the business cycle. Peaks and troughs and the resulting recessions and expansions are normal consequences of economic action. Depression and hyperinflation are not.

CONFESSION

No broker likes to admit his mistakes (even those of us who are retired from the profession) but I believe I owe you an explanation. Brokers tend to be egotistical to begin with because there is so much they need to know. Once comfortable with that knowledge the tendency is to ignore challenging information. I will admit that in a very few cases I did not heed the warning clearly evident in declining fundaments and to compound the problem I ignored the confirmation in the technical charts. One mistake I seldom made was to double up on a bad position. I did very well in the markets but I did make mistakes when I thought my assessment was better than (1) experts who cautioned, (2) decaying fundamentals (3) downside gaps, and broken trend lines. Steel yourself against yourself and realize the markets processes data better than you will.

"WAIT TILL THE SUN SHINES NELLIE"

I look forward to hearing this depression-era refrain every Christmas Eve. It is a song about hope for a better tomorrow. It is sung by the traders on the floor of the New York Stock Exchange near the end of trading. Sometimes it makes me a bit misty eyed; I suppose this is because of my lifelong involvement with the markets as a broker and investor.

Following a particularly bad year in the market, it helps to bring about a sense of closure. I am confident that you have learned enough in these pages to jump start your investing career and at the end of a year you too will learn to love to watch the traders sing this old favorite.

It will please you and you will be anxious and confident as you face the New Year. Incidentally, "Wait Till the Sun Shines Nellie" was written in 1905, the same year that a smart fellow named Einstein began talking about a concept called relativity and gave us the famous equation, $E= MC^2$

I would offer good luck but luck is of little use in the world of investing and is a poor substitute for skill. Instead, you will be successful because you have trained yourself to think in economic terms and because you have the fundamental and technical mindset necessary to make informed and reasoned choices among alternatives.

Relativitely speaking, success is largely beholden to knowledge. I challenge you to learn more. Know your subject. Finally, when you have done well, start to practice singing the lyrics of the old song. Who knows someday you might be singing it on the floor of the NYSE as a broker.

CONCLUSION

I have tried to introduce complicated subject material in an informative and entertaining manner. Some of the points I have made with respect to some products and procedures might be contested by persons in the industry today. I offer them as opinion based upon my considerable experience. During my career, I sold insurance products, stocks, bonds, mutual funds, and commodities. All of these had stringent educational requirements. I do not offer prohibitions lightly.

The new investor must realize that at the starting point he or she is not equipped to consider difficult strategies. A learning curve will develop. The reader is encouraged to utilize available source works such as books, newspapers, and periodicals. Also, I have emphasized the importance of a dual examination of the data relative to an investment choice. I suggest that no such review is complete without study of both fundamental and technical factors.

Technical analysis may seem a bit daunting but it can be very useful even with only a beginner's knowledge. I use fundamental analysis to tell me what to buy or sell and technical analysis to tell me when to buy or sell. Any evaluation of one without the other leaves the analysis incomplete.

This book was not intended to be an in depth presentation of the markets. Instead it was designed to introduce you to the mind set principles that will guide you to a real comfort level as you make choices. As the cover shows reward and risk are related. It will be wise to remember that fact.

Space and cost considerations prohibit me from additional discussion of the dangers of deflation and hyperinflation. The reader is invited to study the Great Depression (deflation) and the hyperinflation of Germany in 1923 and more recently Zimbabwe. I have included a picture of the largest single piece of fiat money of which I am aware. It is essentially worthless and was printed in 2008 in Zimbabwe.

With this piece of currency in mind, we must be ever vigilant to guard against further debasement of our own money.

Please have respect and admiration for your broker. He or she has had to learn much about many aspects of the markets. Many brokers will hold securities, commodities and insurance licenses and will have taken and passed difficult exams. Think of the broker as a buffer between you and the marketplace. An advanced degree such as an MBA or a CFP designation indicates additional study of the markets.

FOLLOW THIS GUIDELINE

From a Latin poem by Horace,

CARPE DIEM

Which means, "Seize the day"

I HAVE ENJOYED TEACHING YOU. MAKE US BOTH PROUD

Suggested Reading List

I strongly recommend a current publication as a mainstay for continuing education. Any of these are excellent sources for study: *Barron's, Investor's Business Daily, Forbes, Fortune, Smart* Money or *Kiplinger's.*

A basic college economics textbook is highly recommended and will help you understand the necessary financial concepts. The Teaching Company of Chantilly, Virginia offers a number of economic courses on DVD. These are taught by some of the best professors in the country.

These few books I list for you are some of the best and earliest I used for my study. Check to see if the book that interests you is still in print.

The Richest Man in Babylon, George S. Clason, Signet Pocket Books, 1988.

How to Make Money in Wall Street, Louis Rukeyser, Doubleday and Company, Inc, Garden City, New York, 1976.

How to Buy Stocks, 8th edition, Louis Engel and Henry R. Hecht, Little Brown and Company, 1994.

Candle Patters—A *Japanese Candle Pattern* Reference *Guide*, Gregory L. Morris, 1999, (pamphlet) from his Basic Candlestick Charting Explained, McGraw Hill, 1995.